# The Girl with No Mouth

Edith Broadwater

Published by Edith Broadwater, 2024.

While every precaution has been taken in the preparation of this book, the publisher assumes no responsibility for errors or omissions, or for damages resulting from the use of the information contained herein.

THE GIRL WITH NO MOUTH

**First edition. January 15, 2024.**

Copyright © 2024 Edith Broadwater.

ISBN: 979-8224219254

Written by Edith Broadwater.

# Table of Contents

Introduction:

I was officially diagnosed first with schizophrenia, and eventually borderline personality disorder. Two serious issues that have corrupted my brain, which is funny because most of my family doesn't even believe in mental illness. (*Just be normal!*)

This book is filled with my delusions, splittings, hallucinations, and dissociation episodes that have haunted me, and although it won't always make sense to the reader, I think that's kind of the point...mental illness doesn't make sense. It's confusing and illogical yet it's all-consuming and if I let it: powerful enough to annihilate the very home that I call my mind.

Some of these episodes I can't distinguish reality from what's inside my head. I experience them as if they're real, and/or have detached myself from reality. They last minutes to hours. Some of them happen after a suicide attempt. The miracle girl, I am she.

Psychosis bleeds into it and me...changing the meaning of what people tell me, their faces, their intentions. A distortion that shimmers and bends reality around me, a being under the surface of the water, but trying desperately to look up to the sky, to the land, to the town, to the people.

The timeline in this book bounces around a little bit. And because even I can't tell sometimes, I decided to not even put in any specific indicators when I am writing about what's in my head or what is happening in the real world. That will be for you to interpret however you see fit. Because this isn't just my mental illness, yet it's still whispered about.

Don't get me wrong: There were times that I was just a bitch or made the wrong choices that I'm not blaming on my mental illness. This doesn't define me, and I don't usually go around telling everyone what's wrong with me.

I am writing this to empty my words into the galaxy, to spill them amongst the stars.

Or in a less pretentious way: to my best friend, to my aunt, to my

3 sisters, to my beautiful partner. Each one helping me in their own way, different periods of times, different, different, different, but so the same.

AND FUCK ANY AND EVERY one that has told me that I don't look 'mentally ill' or that I'm faking. You know exactly who the fuck you are.

# CHAPTER 1

Peeling your skin and dismantling your bones to build someone else a home just leaves you naked and alone. But the feeling of *such goodness* swallows and carries you to a whole new dimension; one that you are so sure that no other being has ever crossed the threshold before, and one that certainly doesn't reek of human decomposition and hatred and vomit.

Is this an acceptable price to pay? Everything that you know, have known, or will know, completely void in the eyes of ...God? The Universe? Would you be willing to drop literally everything to tear off your mortal form at a moment's notice?

Mental illnesses are a real bitch. They sneak in and burrow into your brain and fester and rot it until you are just a husk of a person while everyone else around you are screaming that you're alright! You're alright!

And other times, you're convincing everyone around you that you're fine while knowing inside that you are steadily disintegrating back into the earth and dust and stars from which you come from. Or you're in between and live in an achromic limbo, desperately searching, crawling on your hands and knees, for a colorful oasis to call home for the night.

I have come to terms with the voices in my head and the people that come in and out of my apartment that leave no human trace or emotion. I listen to the abuse and accept it as my own, twisting it until the sharp thorns can't prick me anymore. I'd like to think it hasn't jaded me fully yet, innocence remaining in my breath until the last one, but how am I to judge without biases? Can true purity genuinely live on in a persons' mind while living on this god-forsaken planet?

I have held my tongue for as long as I remember. Too shy, too scared, too small, to speak up. Unable to convey my true emotions lest they be cast aside and spoken into nothingness. And from that silence and unwillingness for caustic inflections, accusations and abuse have covered me from head to toe, coating me in this...disgusting, scarred up tissue. From the people in my life to the voices in my head that no amount of music or medication can drown out. Every minute of my existence, I am plagued with the criminality of a guilty person, all the while, silently screaming to the universe that I am innocent! I am innocent! I *am* innocent!

Wouldn't one argue that if enough people are claiming this as the truth, then that it does become the truth?

And isn't it enough to know that when every single one of us crosses that threshold from life into death, that the truth metamorphoses: from seemingly nothing to right in front of our very own eyes? We are all forced to repent and view our sins one by one, so very alone and so very disheartening. Some more than others.

I have seen too much mental illness in my life—in myself and in other people—to truly believe that the truth will be set free. People believe what they want to believe, and anything you say will be cherry picked to confirm whatever is going on inside their own head. And I am just too tired—too long have I lived—to argue with anybody for much longer.

WAKING INSIDE A HALLUCINATION is an incredibly lonely feeling. The flashing astigmatism lights are blinding, yet I can tell exactly what is going on. Or can I?

I see my grandma walking away. I call for her, crying as I had as a child, begging her to only turn around, to see me. Why won't she turn around? I need her, why is she ignoring me?

My body is weak, my heartbeat is reluctant yet deafening. It's racing to the finish line, eager to stop for the last time. It throbs once. And stops.

A second time. And stops.

Then one final time. And...

Silence.

I'm naked of clothes and sin, incapable of hiding anything. I'm standing in a brilliant star, a firework, a starburst of pigmentation and beauty. A kaleidoscope of alluring colors dazzle me, my eyes unable to fully grasp the foreign hues.

My body feels weightless and beautiful; pain a forgotten memory. My worries evaporate in the snowstorm I am standing in. The tornado. The hurricane. Every single beautiful natural disaster. I am safe in the eye, overlooking the aurora, the Northern Lights. I am a waterfall, a lightning storm, a Garden.

Suddenly, I'm ripped away. Tossed out on the street like trash, run out like I was patient zero. All the pain and hurt of not just me, but all that have lived before and all that will live after me crushing me, squeezing my chest until I could hardly breathe. All the good ceasing to exist, leaving only horrifying, godforsaken anguish. This turmoil churning a thousand times over inside me, devouring anything left inside me.

The face has always been in front of me, never have I ever gotten a break.

I'm rubbing my eyes, but it doesn't disappear. In fact, it gets bigger and starts to morph into another face every time I blink.

I'm mesmerized.

My chest is being crushed down into the bed by an invisible force. I can't move, I'm tied up in an unseeable rope. Limbs trembling and straining to escape, unable to even open my mouth for a sound to come out.

He's coming closer to me. The grin growing larger and more sinister with every step to me, smelling my fear and urine and sweat and blood. I'm feverishly blinking, begging God to make me disappear, or better yet, stop my heart. My body is filled with electricity, but with nowhere to go, zaps only me; every bolt frying my nerves and tendons, boiling my blood and cooking my insides and brain.

I just want this over with.

Please, all of it. All of it.

He's standing over me now. He's still, listening intently to the only sound in the room: my heart beating against my ribcage, threatening to crack bones. His long, slender arm reaches out towards me.

Oh God, oh God, oh God, oh, no.

His sickly skin is hot and cold against my bare chest. I'm screaming so loudly in my head I'm certain that everybody can hear me. Not just me. Not just God.

His fingers graze along my left breast, outlining my heart, preparing to rip it straight out of my vulnerable body.

Oh, his skin. His sickly-sweet stench fills my nostrils and makes me feel as if I'm about to pass out and never wake up.

But this merciless god, this...bystander, would never allow that. I'm immortal, unable to escape this Hell. He pushes down, pushes and pushes and pushes and pushes until my whole abdomen is caved in. I can't inhale, eyes bulging, throat constricted, lungs screaming. His smile is filling my whole vision. That smile, that smile, smile, always smile, smile.

And ever so slowly, he lifts his hand up, fingers trailing the hole he so lovingly created. Up the base of my neck, my lips, nose, until he stops in between my eyes, right below my forehead. And he starts to push again.

But this time even slower.

Slow enough that I can feel every crack and fissure rupture in my skull. I hear the crack as my scalp splits into two. There is no blood; only brains and thoughts spilling out. My vulnerability is deafening, thunderous, revealed to the world.

The moonlight is the only illuminating source. She's laughing at me, with him. My only—or so I thought—friend.

My vision is doubling, the pain quenching my body, never loosening its grip on me and my poor soul. Then he starts to lean down. His face right in front of mine. Nose to nose. He kisses me, his dry cracked lips forcing mine open. He fills my mouth with vomit and blood and dirt.

I cannot breathe.

I cannot swallow.

I must lie there as Death pools in my throat. It starts to leak from my nose, and then my ears, and eyes, and pores. It's burning me, it's killing me.

Oh, God, help me please, please help me.

His eyes focused on mine, feeding in delight. His mouth still suctioned to mine, his hands still caressing my broken body, my vulnerable brain, my still-strong heart, my concave lungs. Please stop touching me, help me.

The amount of pus and bodily fluid leaking from my orifices start to pool around me, threatening to drown me, but maybe I am already drowning. Is this not how drowning feels like? I'm stuck in this moment, every second dragging along, every heartbeat echoing multiple times until the next beat.

My weary heart stutters, unenthusiastically getting back into rhythm.

My body exhausted; my soul aches.

Oh, how my fucking soul aches.

MY EYES OPEN TO THE white walls of a hospital. I'm handcuffed to the bed, padding on the rails so I don't hurt my head. My body is my own again, at least for the moment, and I slowly stretch out my limbs. As hospital policy, there is a nurse sitting by the door, guarding me against the world. She looks up from her phone, giving me a warm smile. She asks if I need anything to drink or eat. It's disconcerting being back in reality, but I welcome it. I accept it, I accept the food, I accept the help, and she tells me that I've been in the ER for 4 days.

They pumped my stomach and started me on antipsychotics. Something to do with charcoal? She talks slowly and extra sweetly, but I still cannot understand her. Her words fly out of her mouth, and I watch as they hit the ceiling and disappear, puffs of multicolored smoke. Pink, green, orange... There are a few typos and grammatical errors that I so desperately want to correct but have already reached the heavens and disappeared to where I could not, so alas.

I can smell my own sweat and body odor, a repulsive reminder that I am back in existence. Now that I'm awake and my stomach is clean, they can find the closest available bed in the mental hospital for me. The wheeling of my bed down the hall is the most humiliating moment of my life, and I cringe every time someone darts quickly to move out of the way.

While not their intention, I feel paraded and the center of attention when we get to the building. Intake is the same at every hospital, and they finally leave me alone in my room to shower and wash the puke, stench, and unholiness off of me.

Ghosts walk up and down the hallways, murmuring amongst themselves. Time is meaningless in a place like this. The fluorescent lights pale and expose skeletons, the embodiment of melancholy and hopelessness in a place that has been long forgotten by the real world. I can't tell if I'm truly here or not. Maybe this isn't real. Maybe I'm not real.

Faces around me are constantly morphing, always laughing. My chest is heavy and hard to move, my lungs scream for air. Just one more breath. I just need one more breath. Inhaling too quickly closes my throat, threatening to stay adhered forever. Exhaling feels as if I'm releasing pieces of my soul that I so desperately need.

Colors explode into confetti and dazzle my already tired eyes. The voices are beautiful, enticing me as a siren calls to the inferior sailor. They know how exhausted I am. They can hear it, for my aching bones scream to anybody who stops to listen.

My mind is full, and my body is empty. I have nothing. I was shattered and taken apart, setting up my bones and ripping the skin off my body to shelter my bleeding corpse from the cold, from the wind, from the faces. Every slice of me, every crudely ripped piece of me, dripping in sweat and blood, leaving a trail of metaphorically depraved breadcrumbs.

My body was not my own, but a home for others, sacrificing everything I had (which was nothing) for them. My emotions, actions, thoughts, memories, all visible for the world to discern and judge, to be picked apart and left strewn carelessly all throughout time and space.

I'm on my knees, praying to anything and anyone that would listen. Please, please, please set me free. Wasn't my whole life leading up to this moment? I've seen the signs, the hints, the warnings. I felt that I was finally understanding yet being punished arbitrarily once again.

Every day here is the same: eating when they place food in front of me, taking the medication that the group of uninterested and indifferent male doctors have prescribed me. They hear the words 'confused' and 'delusional', and they siphon antipsychotics into me while their eyes rake over my hospital gown and any unintentionally exposed skin that may be peeking out. Their stares pierce into me and I always feel that sharp prick of shame, anxiety, and fear permeate into my soul, burning into me and leaving me feeling tainted...dirty...unpure.

And then they move on to the rest of their day, wherever that might be. I suspect that they disappear from existence the moment they leave my sight.

Reality is slippery and difficult for me to keep a firm grasp on. Logically, I can think reasonable thoughts and try to ease my mind, but the fear and paranoia is too strong and so overwhelming that it glazes my perception and chokes me. What's real? What's in my head? What can I trust?

Slowly, I am brought back into the real world. Gone are the monsters from my vision—at least temporarily—and back into my head where they belong. I participate in group therapy because I know that that is the fastest way to get out of here.

Pretend that you're better.

Pretend that you're normal again.

I smile at the nurses and the doctors hiding behind the counters. I make friends and we all try to convince the other person that we aren't in here because we're crazy!

There are hundreds, thousands, millions of signs around us from the universe, and most people ignore them. Or maybe they just don't know that something is trying to communicate with them. But with medication, the signs dwindle and the once grand devotion from the cosmos abate into desolate silence that leaves a sour taste in my mouth.

With the medication comes less emotion and less noise in my head. My own personal sliver of goodness is dulled, but that just means I'm more capable of existing in this so-called real world. I don't know which is a better existence: a life of a divinity that is unheard and misunderstood or a life of consistent mediocrity and insipid palpability.

How much skin do I shed to satisfy heedless mortals?

# CHAPTER 2

It was the coldest I had ever been in my life, walking around in the middle of the night with nothing but a few sweaters on, a duffle bag of a few clothes I couldn't leave behind. I was trying to check in the mental hospital that I had been at before, but they had no room for me and weren't interested in trying to help me. I was too ashamed to go back to my grandparents, knowing that I would just hurt and disappoint them if I was half present again. Disappoint, disappoint, disappoint. Whatever direction I go: disappoint, disappoint, disappoint...

The voices were so overwhelming and powerful that there were times I couldn't tell if I had had a real conversation with a person or if I had imagined the whole scene. I would be walking down a sidewalk in the middle of downtown when all of a sudden, I'd be in the middle of a lake. The only things real were my feet and the bag on my shoulder.

He wasn't any better than me; stuck in his head and when he came back, savagely lashing out in fear. My feet followed him, listening to him rambling on about nonsense that only made sense to him.

I would try to walk away from him, and he'd follow me, berating and yelling until he saw someone stick their head out of their house, and he'd turn into a child, begging me to walk alongside him so that he wouldn't be arrested. Kneeling on his knees to apologize, face wet from tears and snot, I could only nod my head at this...werewolf.

I couldn't tell the difference between the man in my head and my partner. *Folie à deux,* madness of two, intoxicating and impossible to leave.

Nobody ever talks about mental illnesses besides depression and anxiety, I didn't fully understand why I was feeling and seeing the way that I was. Doesn't mental illness mean where you're stuck in bed all day? Doesn't it mean unlimited support from your family, doesn't it mean getting better after a few days or weeks or months? Doesn't it mean help, because I have lost myself and I don't even know how to ask for help because what do I need help for? What's wrong with me? What am I?

One foot in front of the other for hours. My body hurt, my head asleep, nothing ever still and nothing never not doing their job. But if I stopped, something bad would happen. Days, weeks, seconds—time—blended into a mix of snow, and rain, and mud pooling in the bottom of my shoes but still, I continued on. The less energy I had, the more he had, sucking mine and giving him the strength to walk ahead occasionally or dance around me trying to egg me on.

He stole my phone and refused to give it back on the fourth day and that was my breaking point. I was so tired that I didn't care about anything, including him, and I ran from him and once I had lost him for good, I went to go find a spot (ironically enough: behind the building of the mental hospital that had turned me away). Privacy. I need trees, not people. I need to lay down as Pan and say that the great god is dead.

The first time I laid down in days, the first rest that I truly had in all my existence! Look how lovely the red and orange leaves are! Shimmering in the sunlight, glinting as if a thousand brilliant gems were adhered to the tree branches. Hosting a private, bewitching dance in the gentle breeze; Mother Nature's crowned jewels.

The sun was blazing that morning, a silent apology for freezing me the last couple nights. Illinois October nights would dip down below the 20s. I had been so cold for so long that my body no longer shivered and bare skin didn't protest the bite of the wind anymore.

Children laughing and screaming echo in my ears, as loud as church bells. Cars revving in the distance, forever in a hurry, hurry, hurry. Dogs barking into the breeze, street vendors yelling, doors slamming. How much of it was real and how much of it was in my head? I couldn't even think logically at this point, and still have no idea to this day how much bustling background was made up in the soundtrack of my head.

It's funny how gray and dull the world is until the moment you decide to leave. I spent days walking around in a monotone, dismal limbo—never seeing color in its true form.

I was so lost in my thoughts that I didn't immediately notice someone standing in front of me. It's my teenage sister. But—how...? She lives hours away.

"Whatcha doin?"

She wore loose clothing despite the cold, sunlight dancing on her dark hair and creating shadows that changed her facial expressions every couple of seconds. She was stagnant, a force so calm that I felt compelled to tell her the truth, even though it was difficult to look her in the eye and divulge in the societal taboo that's been on my mind since day one.

"I'm tired. I don't want to do this anymore."

I spoke out loud, although I knew if I chose not to, she would still be able to understand me. Out of the corner of my eye, I see the rest of my family. My dad was right there, my aunt, my papa, my baby cousin. Everybody was barefoot yet they weren't bothered by the cold. I desperately wanted to get up and give my sweater to my grandma, but she motioned for me to stay. We formed a circle, with our knees not quite touching the others. How did they all find me?

"You know what you have to do." The voice coming from my dad was both not his and his. Everyone nodded to my left where the two bottles of miscellaneous pills were already out and opened. Which one of them had pulled them out from the bottom of my duffle bag?

Obediently, I took each pill. Popping them like candy, talking and laughing with my loved ones as we had years ago before hubris had ruptured our family, splitting them forever. Their laughter rang out, thundering in the distance and chasing out the depression that had choked the whole country—nay, the world. I didn't feel the cold anymore or the hard ground under me. My feet and legs didn't ache anymore, and I felt my spirit become renewed. I was a child again, and to see my family happy like this, years before desolation had emerged and stolen their kaleidoscopic colors, was a gift that I gratefully accepted.

How long we were out there, I have no idea, because time didn't exist in that moment.

When I started seeing double and then prismatic triple, my grandma laid me down, my head in her lap. I looked up at her, and although I saw fear in her eyes, I suspect it was just reflecting my own. My body felt both heavy and light, like I would float into the sky if she let go of me but sink straight to the bottom of the ocean. With all their eyes on me, I didn't want to worry them, so I kept my face neutral. My baby sister gave me one more hug, tight enough that it nearly choked me, and Papa gave me a hand squeeze.

Touching their skin one last time gave me the confidence that I needed, and I closed my eyes.

ALL I SEE IS AN ENDLESS blue. Blue water, blue sky, blue hell. Not a cloud in sight, not a wave to disturb, as if to taunt me. The small wooden boat bobs ever so slightly, stability long gone, a distant memory. My skin is freshly pink, turning red. I want the cool relief that I know will come by jumping into the water, but I am afraid and unsure if I am able to embrace a bittersweet compromise with the devil himself.

A man comes and goes, showing himself sometimes to me. He keeps me company, and although I tried my very best in the beginning to ignore him, to avoid giving him the attention he so desperately craves, alas, I would have gone mad years ago if not for him. He appears when my lungs close, when I bleed from my eyes, or when I'm frantically brushing the bugs off my burnt skin, scraping layers off until I can see muscle and bone. Yet, the bugs are still there, dancing around and taunting me, leaving me no choice but to stick my fingers in between my tendons and try to pick them out. I never catch them.

He laughs, but maybe not at me, I think. Perhaps I am just funny, but fail to see the humor. After all, a human life means nothing, and I am just a speck of stardust on this godforsaken hunk of earth.

I ask him why we're here. Why are we here on this boat in the middle of limbo? He never answers, just deliberately stares back as if I know the answer already. Maybe I do.

Am I even alive? Am I dead? Did I exist at all in the first place?

As much as I try, I cannot even remember my life prior to this hell. Maybe if I were to slip into the water, as it beckons, there are answers.

I dip a toe in reluctantly, and the air starts to color, suffocating and urging me to inhale the water that I am sure my body will know how to breathe. I'm almost certain I've been on this boat for ages, this is the only home I know now. Isn't it?

I jump off the boat as hard as I can, creating a colossal wave—one that feasibly, I'm sure, initiates the great big bang that births the universe. Bubbles surround me, dizzying and ensuring that I don't know for sure which way is up. I hold my breath until I feel as if my lungs are about to pop. I kick aimlessly, dismally aiming for the surface. The salt burns my skin, but it's an emotion that reminds me that I am here. Wherever that is. I am a person. This pain tells me that I am a person.

My head breaks the surface, and I tread lightly while the man stares at me from that crudely made boat. He smiles and I know that I made the right choice. Something tugs at my feet, and I kick out of reflex, but it grabs me again. I feel the five fingers, but when I look down—woe is me—I cannot see anything.

Then another hand grabs my other flailing foot. Do I let go? The man is smiling, oblivious. But is he? Isn't he the one down there grabbing me?

My fear is bleeding into the water. My eyes stay on him, unable to look away. He nods once. I know. I freeze, my limbs becoming limp, from dread, from the cold, from my own discretion, I can't tell.

The strong hands pull me under. My arms float above my head and as I look up at that dreadful, deviled sun, my fingers are the last to kiss the air. It's peaceful under the water without the disarray of bubbles. It's dark and calm, no sounds or movements. The hands continue to descend, and the lower I go, the calmer I feel. The air is escaping my lungs, but I do not feel fear or panic. I'm escaping limbo.

My lungs hurt and I instinctually take a breath, filling in with salt water instead of air. It burns, oh, God, it burns, and I almost start to fight, but my body is going limp without my control. This is the only way out. The water becomes colder and darker, but alas, I am free.

When I become aware of my existence, I'm able to look around in this pitch-black room. I was alone. I've always been alone. I've never seen anything in the light; my whole life I've wasted my so-called eyes. My body cries every day for any kind of sustenance that I just lack resources, or maybe just the motivation, to obtain.

But then there's a small white orb floating in the air. It comes closer to me, bobbing gently, whispering my name, enticing me to come closer.

Do I dare?

I take minutes, hours, days, weeks, even years to take a step closer.

And another. And another.

Until I'm right in front of it, my pupils aching, heating my skin and face as it never has been before.

I reach out and touch it with one hesitant finger. It sizzles and burns out, my disappointment falling in so quickly it chokes me.

But then I'm encompassed in white light once again. The heat. The brightness. It hurts but feels so good.

There's a woman standing in front of me, light emitting from her long slender body, white dress flowing and rippling as if underwater.

She doesn't speak, only puts a finger up to her lips and points to the middle of the room behind me.

I turn, startled, as a firework explodes. A fire roars to life, larger than the sun, touching the once dark ceiling, expelling all shadows and cobwebs that once haunted my very soul. The fire is beautifully transcendent, full of colors: blue, purple, gold, colors that were usually unseen by the human eye but have gifted to me their existence.

The lady glides to the fire, reaching her bare arms inside. She grabs the flame, wrestling it until it tames, wrapping its dragon-like body as ribbons all around her being. She dances, the flame and color mesmerizing, captures the sparkles and auroras. Her body is as graceful as a shooting star, twisting and turning the fire as if it's always been an extension of her soul since the beginning of time.

Beings come to life, worshipping her, serenading her, filling the room with love and life. She is contagious. It is a beautiful chaos in this once empty room, and the loneliness is an obliterated feeling that no longer exists in the entire world.

I start to move in ways that I have never, body aching and cracking, urging me to give up and keep wallowing in depression and darkness, but I sway regardless. I twirl, I laugh, I smile. The fire growing to all around the room, filling in the gaps and cracks.

Her lips aren't moving but I can hear her sing, her voice ranges higher than the mountains and thundering deeper than the ocean. Iridescent bubbles and smoke and wisps of fire and music fill my soul, empty for so long, unknowingly yearning all these years for this very moment.

She is beautiful, once chameleoning into the mysterious jungles and forests and Mother Nature herself but now unashamed and basking in this divine moment.

The fire grazes me, needing permission. I grant it my life and it devours me. I'm swallowed whole, into the belly of a whale; an endless, bottomless pond, a waterfall of exile. I raise my arms, bearing the mark of the cross and I know that I will, finally, be at peace. I know that she will never leave my side, I'm finally safe from the pain and hunger and cold. Will it be worth all of the past suffering? From life to life, to ash to dust to everything to absolutely nothing at all to this meat vessel I bid home? To the brief moments of pleasure to the eternity lasting agonizing spitting of God himself?

The answer lies in the colored fire, wrapping my essence like a present, which extinguishes just as quickly as it all started. I am left with starburst eyes and a lone presence that halts their movements.

Graced upon my mortal form, the celestial calm whose immured facade of unholy and sick bloom in my tamed heart. It's not an unpleasant feeling, yet its foreign despair and anew aura lift what's left of my soul. There is no fear of the figure in my corner. And although I had just spent decades watching her dance and sing, I could not recall who she was or what she even looked like. In the new dark, she has a completely different physical body. She is merely watching, and I feel like a science experiment kept behind glass to protect those who had created me without truly understanding the consequences.

Dark eyes forbearingly studying all that is happening, nothing escaping from her gaze; not judging, uncriticizing. She is so unlike any other being I have ever seen—her face so beautiful it would be debased if I were to try to describe it in any crude or obscene human language.

When she steps closer, the air in my fatigued lungs expels and then struggles to fill back up. As if I were Narcissus and she was my reflection, forever dooming me to stare as my own flesh and bones melt and disintegrate into the earth from which I emerged from.

Her tongue is not in any human dialect, but I understand each word. She is asking if I am ready. But my youth betrays me, whispering of hope, a small glimmer of candlelight that is so nonexistent to me but lights up the whole performance (truly unbeknownst to me).

Grief and jaded disgust cloud my living ghost, parading its diseased misery to pervert...me. For too long I have endured and mistakenly missed all three of my...infinite...kisses. Wings of feather baptizing my ailing self, persuading me to lean in and cease all there is to me.

The first: I came willingly. Drifting lazily, afresh with desire, and I was brought back. The second, I kissed, but did not close my eyes. And what does that say about me? As a person? As a lover? As a child?

And the third. Oh, the third. I did all right, but it was her, this time, that turned her cheek towards the Heavens! The ultimate cosmic joke, the only reason the universe was created and the only reason the universe has sustained for all these millennia. For this appalling moment—the humiliation and degradation of reaching to the iridescent and opalescent stars up above only to be intercepted by a knowing parent entity. Do I accept this? Or is my life's ultimate ambition to gaze upon this virtuosity of death without consequence?

*But it isn't always like this*, she silently reminds me. The unfeeling, unwelcoming cold that has welded to the bottom of my soul, dragging me into this pit that I am so, so, so afraid of. My skin has a complexion of a man that has realized his immortality is being threatened, or an animal that has been backed into a corner and is desperately looking around for its chance of survival.

I have no secrets from her, yet I feel ashamed. She crosses the small dark room; the only light source is a small fire in the corner opposite from me. She's in front of me and my soul straightens up. My skin feels less hot, but it's difficult to read her. Is she disappointed? Angry? Sad?

She reaches up as if to stroke my cheek, heat blazing from my skin. I imagine I can almost hear an audible sizzle when her cold fingers lightly brush me. Forehead to cheek, cheek to chin. Eye contact steady, unwilling to let me go of this nonexistent standoff we are in. Her touch is soothing...and then suddenly it turns ugly. I feel her fingers start to dig into me, like a kid playing with Play-Doh. Up to her first knuckle, the pain is searing and loud, freezing me into place and unable to lift my arms or even to move my body to protect myself. Gaping holes melted into my skin, scarring me permanently. My mouth opens in a silent howl, I'm screaming, yet still holding eye contact.

*I trusted you! I trusted you! I trusted you!*

I wanted to yell, but no words could form, and my incompetent tongue refused to obey. Her expression has not changed, but I could see myself in the reflection from her eyes. My eyes, wild and red, unblinking in the wake of her horror. Drool dripping, for I am too inhumane to swallow, nothing more than a common bitch. Blood and flesh fall from my face, four fingernail craters left on each side of my face. I can see the muscles of my cheeks, flexing and moist as tears pool up only to be washed away by blood. The sound of her dropping loose and broken skin hitting the ground is deafening, squelching loudly as if to mock me for being weak. Her hands are cradling my face, eyes studying my expressions, following each drop of blood—or is it tears? —without remorse or regret. The spell not yet fully unbroken, I fall to my knees, head held high towards the heavens and towards her.

Why is she doing this to me? What have I done to be punished like this? Every sin I have committed plays in my head, small to recent—from stealing that fake flower at the store all the way to the thoughts and vindictive revenge that echo around in my head.

*But that isn't me! This isn't fair! I am not that person!*

But the gaping holes in my face contradict me, telling—no, showing—me how wrong I am. This *is* me. This *is my fault.* I am being punished because that is all I deserve. I deserve every single composition of pain that has been inflicted on anybody and everybody in the past, present, and future. I feel it all and could only embrace it, *accept* it as my own. But will she kill me? No, that isn't how she conveys her message. I am left alive, unfortunately, and even though she is the one who has burned me alive, when her arms open up, I crawl into them, submissive as a child. My blood still on the hands that are cradling me and brushing away my tears, carefully maneuvering around my open wounds. She offers no words or explanations, but I knew.

# CHAPTER 3

It's a brand-new fear opening your eyes after you were sure that you'd be dead. Am I still on Earth, my head, or the afterlife? My whole body hurts as if I'd been hit by a monstrous force and rendered me dumbstricken. And of course—as sure as the sun rises in the morning—the eternal white walls greet me as an old friend.

My left-hand throbs and is swollen to three times its normal size, and I'm unable to unclench it. Later, I'd find out I damaged a nerve in my arm that would require multiple doctor visits and referrals, and eventually surgery.

"Do you know how lucky you are?"

Every time I'm in this situation, it's always that question that burns the inside of my skin. As if I were in control enough to stop this tidal wave of depression and trouble that sweeps everyone off their feet and drowns them without a second thought. Our definitions of lucky are so distant that it's practically another language they're speaking in.

They try to disgustingly justify it by telling me I'm attractive, young, I have the whole world in my hands, how bright my future could be if I would just be normal. As if I am choosing this way of life. I've never had a doctor or nurse sit down and actually listen to me. And I can't fault them for that; they don't have the time to listen to the tales of woe spun by one girl. They offer the generic help: exercise, eat right, get therapy, medicine, medicine, medicine.

I'm staring at the three gray glove boxes that are hanging up on the wall in front of me. Small, medium, large. The medium box is presenting a man's face appearing to escape. His face is sad, wrinkled yet not from age, but maybe just emotion. His eye sockets are empty and wistful, his mouth is open in a silent cry. From what, I do not know. He speaks so softly that I cannot hear him, but the sorrow is heavy in the air. He turns slightly away, as if in shame. He talks for a long time, content to spill his secrets to only the universe, the only presence that is logically able to receive his words. Perhaps I am just an intruder in his private conversation, but this doesn't stop me from straining my ears to try to listen.

Next to him is only a mouth. A woman's feminine mouth, a man's mouth, a baby's mouth, my mouth. It's wide open, with two fingers jammed into it, pulling the jaw down, an endless struggle whose winner is not apparent. Are the fingers trying to escape from the throat or are they trying to enter? They battle and clash and fight yet no matter how long I watch, there is never an end.

When the man has said all he has needed to, his mouth starts to widen, his jaw dropping almost all the way to the floor, engulfing the room and swallowing the light. Instead of agony, it is replaced with fury and hatred. Instead of words, he only screams. It is so loud that it shatters my eardrums, blood dripping down onto my shoulders and down my arms and hands. I am paralyzed with fear and am unable to cover my ears, forced to sit and absorb this gray man's torments. Too long this goes on, I am afraid that I'm now forever poisoned.

When the nurse gets up from her chair at the door, the spell is broken, and I am able to move again. My ears are still ringing, and I have to ask her to repeat herself. When she is ready to draw my blood, she pulls out gloves from the medium box, taking away the man and his unearthly screams. After she sits back down, I notice that the box is now showing a man's naked back and butt. I am uncomfortable, and I make a point to not look in that direction again.

They prepare to take me to the mental hospital, and once again, I am wheeled and paraded. Intake:

*Do you want to kill yourself?*

*Do you feel like hurting yourself?*
*Do you feel like hurting others?*
Well, considering I came in from another suicide attempt, you tell me.

Unless I'm in the hospital after a suicide attempt, they—more likely male doctors—like to argue with me about if I have the correct diagnosis or if I truly need the medicine I'm asking for. If I ask for a specific medication, one that I'm currently taking or one that has worked in the past, I am told that it won't work, and they don't want to prescribe it and try to persuade me into something else.

Maybe I'm only depressed? I'm in school, right? I'm probably stressed alongside hormonal issues. I have birth control? That's probably it.

Where is my antidepressant for when the world is gray and inanimate and I can barely get out of bed to feed my cat? I'm already skinny yet I've lost 30 lbs. these couple months that I can't afford to lose. Where is my antipsychotic for when I hear singing and voices telling me to kill myself? Where is my mood stabilizer so that I don't go off the rails when I get triggered from the smallest thing, something that reminds my deep conscience of a past trauma but to the naked eye: just an ember, a spark of fire, easily extinguishable. Where the fuck is an anxiety medication that is going to calm my heavy, heavy, heavy heart and let me feel like a person that isn't about to be dropped off the sears building almost every single waking moment?

Trying to convey this to doctors...

Why do I have to fight so hard for all my medicine? I, too, hate taking them. The politeness that I have been raised on, this quietness that I must maintain, must be too quiet and the doctors just don't understand how terrible I feel...all the time...trying to describe a panic attack or a split and the emotions that lead up or follow afterwards is met with an uninterested nod and the next generic question that is on their sheet—the only way they can barely even remember my name.

I just can't seem to convey my emotions and so my emotions are stuck inside me, bleeding me dry because nobody can understand because I cannot explain it but when I try to explain it nobody will listen and I cannot explain it because nobody is listening and...

They look at me and think that an antihistamine in lieu of a real medication will treat my anxiety. Needing high doses for almost everything, yet reaching the usual middle point, and always hearing the same thing:

*Are you sure?*

*Maybe it just needs more time.*

*I think you'll be fine.*

And I fear that once I start spilling, I won't be able to stop the tsunami of hurt and consternation that has been flourishing inside me since before I was born, before I was conceived, before I was a speck of dust in the universe. I am merely a vessel, and I don't want this put back out into the melody of the cosmos, lest I be tarnishing Mother Nature herself.

They can't or don't or won't understand that I have Pandora's box and instead of unleashing the horrors onto the world, I need to swallow the key, the heartbreak, and a bottle of pills. Escaping, but really: living.

Being back in the real world, or at least as real as it can be in the mental hospital, reminds me to act normally so I can be discharged as soon as possible. I remember to keep the voices inside me and my legitimate feelings to myself, presenting as every other normal person. Because mental hospitals are for life threatening emergencies, not ongoing treatment. But Once I'm inside the belly of the beast, it's no longer a life-threatening emergency and I am fine, I am fine.

As soon as they slap a bracelet on me and enter my info into the system... I cease to exist. I am a ghost. It does not matter what I say or do. Nobody can hear me. Nobody can see me. I am not real. I am not real.

The nurses are kind, but even they look straight through me. Nobody can hear my words or answers, so truly, it does not matter.

This treatment team is composed of 9 different people, yet the only acknowledgment is a quick glance when the nurse bringing me in introduces me to everyone. This is nothing but their break time. They are all on their phone, texting, scrolling.

Only one lady looks at me and she smiles and is gentle so whenever I see them, I only speak to her. I only say thank you to her and I only say goodbye to her.

I am a ghost, but I didn't know that at first, and some parts of me still don't believe it, because I can still touch things. I bleed, I eat, I sleep. But everyone is telling me that I am a ghost, so I must be.

In all the mental hospitals I have been in, I don't think there's been a single one-on-one therapy session.

*Do you feel like hurting yourself?*

*Do you feel like hurting someone else?*

*Do you feel like killing yourself?*

The fucking answers don't mean anything. They check off the boxes on their sheets, writing generic notes until they can move onto the next person.

What do you mean, crazy? I have no thoughts of suicide! I don't hear voices! I am here on Earth with you! Please don't keep me here any longer or I'm about to melt into this floor out of boredom!

And I know it's bullshit because refusing to see the treatment team and choosing to sleep instead, and then walking up and down the long hallway and ranting and occasionally yelling...after days and maybe weeks of being there, they let me go the next day. Did they hear my anger? Did they remember that I'm a person? Did the Heavens reach out and decide to push my release?

The more time I spend in here the crazier I am, the crazier I get, and I must be crazy because everyone is telling me so. Right?

# CHAPTER 4

The sun is blinding.

I cannot open my eyes long enough to look around. My pupils are on fire. The sky and land are one, blending together in a union of heat and misery. There is nothing in sight.

No trees, no water, no oasis.

But there is a man off in the distance. As he comes closer, I can see that he is naked and sunburnt and dripping in sweat, dirt and sand. His hair is soaked and sticking up in every direction. His feet are black and cracked; the once soft skin blistered and calloused. His body is tired and dirty and wounded and dehydrated.

But his eyes!

As bright as the sun herself, as warm as coffee, as alive as can be.

He tries to speak to me, his cracked lips bleeding as they pry open, his Adam's apple bobbing up and down, no sound escaping. His emaciated arms wave around weakly, seemingly trying to grasp my attention.

He falls to his knees, white hot sand burning his legs, yet he does not feel pain anymore.

I am afraid to touch him, even the gentlest of touches would split his paper-thin skin into pieces. He would disintegrate into ash, ceasing to exist in this world and the next.

I kneel in front of him and raise to his lips my greatest wealth.

The man guzzles the liquid with a vengeance, as if he were a foal straight from the mother's womb tasting the world for the first time. His eyes closed; he smiles as brightly as the sun-glinted sand. His face softer, filled with hope and light, his shoulders less hunched; no longer carrying the weight of the sky.

Still dripping with water, he looks up at me and slowly leans closer to me.

Thinking he is going to speak, I do the same, ears straining, until our skin touch.

He is surprisingly cool, as if he were standing in a shadow on a nice spring day. I feel his lips press against my cheek one time, three times, nine times. He is thanking me, not just for the water, but for the motivation. For a will to keep going. How does a man sink this low? Practically begging for the end, knowing his life has plateaued enough to greet Death as an old friend.

How long has he been in this God-forsaken desert? How long has he gone without food or water? Without human contact or compassion? Has he passed by haughty people, people thinking they're too good to kneel on their knees in front of him or has he been completely alone, devoid of any signs of life?

I grab his hands and pull him gently to his feet. He's stronger, his skin more color, his eyes impossibly brighter than before.

He stands tall, limbs no longer quivering from exhaustion. He kisses my cheek.

He is a man again. And with the temporary strength that the liquid ambrosia has given him, he chooses to act out in sin and not to uphold the obligation of humanity that one would normally assume after being saved from the brink of death. The monsters escape from his subconsciousness, and he allows it to contaminate and pollute him, and everything he touches afterwards is unsanitary and impure.

I couldn't see it, or maybe I just wouldn't see it.

Not often could I truly grasp the idea that this is real life. It's all fictitious to me.

Previous evils in my life, even when happening to me, didn't really happen to me; it was a screen that I could turn off at any moment. I didn't have to live through this, I could just escape from this universe.

This wasn't my real life; this is akin to an internet avatar that someone would play in the meta universe.

I have heard over and over how people with mental illnesses aren't responsible for how they act. When does that start to apply? After they've spilt innocent blood and before they rid themselves of half their soul or is it before lashing out to all who dare touch them but after we learn the whole story and absolve them?

I didn't understand (and perhaps still not able to fully comprehend) such anger that decays all around husks masquerading as a human, myself included. Although they speak and act as a human, there is something...demonic about them. Everyone. Me. At what point does this leviathan bleed into your true persona?

I hold him closer and closer until he can't bear the touch of my searing skin and has to push himself away. Such evil cannot permit intimation to grace, for it melts away layers of his 'skin' and the nakedness and vulnerability that presents is so terrifying and overwhelming that it chokes his very airway. To be so eroded and decayed and corrupt is a sin itself, but ultimately not a surprise to all who dare look closer.

And as cliche as it sounds, maybe it was the brokenness that beckons me, urging me to come patch it up so that he may shatter it once it's dry. Some people are just born natural destroyers, and the chaos that follows suit is only an essential, yet foul, role in the ecosystem we call our lives.

Or maybe it's my overcompensation for trying to live amongst physical beings and dealing with all those explosions in my head that I give people who don't necessarily deserve chances, chances. I justify it by saying that I have mental health issues and I would be devastated if the people in my life decided to abandon me because of it. I drown myself in order to keep ungrateful people afloat, and while I sit in the dark crushing water, sitting amongst the sandbank surrounded by fish and lost dreams (—delusions?—), there is nothing keeping me company and nothing to keep me afloat.

Frustration builds up inside me, caking my insides and leaving this grimy and greasy residue that coats my organs and slows it all down, unknowing to all glancing past yet is glaringly obvious to me. I feel as if I glow in the dark and passing spacecrafts can spot me in a heartbeat. This feeling of screaming in the middle of the room but nobody even bats an eye. I howl at the moon and the stars but nothing answers. Why isn't my truth heard? Why isn't it bouncing from the mountaintops and spearing any who dare to get in the way of it? Is it in my head?

Why is it when I call the police and tell them about being attacked, with bruises on my skin and bite marks on my chest, with the flesh hanging off my body and the broken window and cracked phone screens that corroborate with my story...why is it that nothing happens? He didn't go to jail for assaulting me that night. He didn't face any repercussions for annihilating my soul and disintegrating my mortal being. And maybe because of this, I came to terms that it wasn't that bad, that I was exaggerating it in my head. He didn't *really* punch, kick, bite, or strangle me, it was all in my head. It's always all in my head.

Why is it when multiple people in multiple apartments call for domestic disputes that nothing happens, except a police officer telling me that if I stole his phone, I better give it back.

*I can search this whole apartment and if I find out you're lying, you'll be in bigger trouble.*

Fucking do it, then. I don't know where the fuck that phone is. I don't ever touch it. Why is it that he was the one yelling for hours, yet I'm the one being accused of causing all this drama?

Search this apartment!

Search me!

I'm not the one yelling and threatening. I'm not the one that caused the next-door neighbors to move out. I'm not the fucking thief, liar, abuser, or user.

My savings: $16,000, all gone because of him. My emergency $1000 cash: stolen when I went on vacation. Car, gaming console, watch, tablet...sold, ruined, 'stolen'.

Nothing done from the law, so again, it must be in my head. It's always in my head. Apparently, it's legal to yell and throw things and damage things in an apartment. Apparently, it's not legal to try to kick an abuser out because of squatter rights' until you give them an official eviction notice.

And 30 days is a short time to wait, huh? Only 30 days more of living with someone who yells at the top of his lungs every single morning, some afternoons, and most nights. Only 30 more days of living with someone who steals cleaning supplies from god-knows-where and permeates the whole apartment, the whole building, reeking it of bleach or vinegar.

Only 30 more days...only 30 more. I couldn't last those 30 days, though, and tried to kill myself again. The constant fear, exhaustion, and frustration is really draining, and it's hard to think straight. I needed help, yet nobody would help me. I needed help, I needed it.

But must be in my head—exaggerated—because if it was truly bad, something would have happened, something would have improved.

Right?

I could avoid taking responsibility and blame my upbringing and family. My stepmom abused my father and I, both in different and in similar ways. My uncle verbally berates my gorgeous aunt even in the midst of company, which leaves me wondering how miserable he makes her in their home life. Isn't this all I know? The curse of the Broadwaters—only a few escape it. Wasn't lying in bed as a child, listening to my stepmom yell and insult my dad, just a training exercise that I'll utilize later in life? I was taught that words are just that. Besides, I already have one screaming man in my head, what's another one?

I have no blood to bleed, and my heart is thickened. They mean nothing to me. I can't even say that I hate because that's too strong of an emotion that just isn't there for me like it used to be. Or maybe it never was, and I just have always been pretending my whole life. How to tell the difference between real emotion and pretend....?

This...nothingness...surrounds me and I've been crouched down pretending to cough and choke, because that's what everyone else would be doing, right? But this is my home, and in this eye of the storm, this cloud of destruction and venom, is where I am most comfortable.

Do I keep pretending not to be able to see out of politeness for others or do I just keep standing? It isn't touching me; I loathe the feeling of it on my skin. I thrive on this chaos and challenge anyone who thinks they can stand here without smoke swelling up their throat and killing them on the spot.

I can survive, not because I am tough, but because I don't really exist. I am not here, and so the smoke cannot hurt me.

And it's fair to say that everyone is broken into pieces of their past, yet not all can assemble or fix it in an artful way that doesn't slice the skin of all who dare touch it. Because all this glass was once beautiful and pure, and when it's inevitably broken, that crack in the surface is forever there. Maybe it's a human norm to think of them as imperfect and ugly, but there is always the free will to transform it to something that doesn't bleed the hands that try to save you.

The people that are able to take all the shit and rage and fury and ...absorb and disappear it from existence, are the real artists of the world. Turning vile into beauty that the world actually wants to see is a feat that is exalted and celebrated by every virtuous being. Because no matter how many people tell you to let it all out or that they're here for the mentally ill, the moment that shit hits the fan, they're gone. And you can't really blame them for not wanting to be splattered.

# CHAPTER 5

I feel as if I'm constantly on a stage in front of an audience. They know that I don't know that I'm being watched, and they've grabbed their popcorn and have stuffed their mouths silly. They love it: the feeling of dread that logically should only be present to me, the audience is still able to somehow sense how palpable it is, thick in the air that drowns me yet only gives them more reason to continue watching.

People around me are only actors and disappear from reality once they pass the curtains. They know their script and enjoy watching me bumble around and (poorly) ad lib my lines. The people on my phone are not real. The texts I receive from friends are purely my imagination and an elaborate hoax set up by the universe to convince me that I am here. Pictures I have must have been faked, and the memories carefully cultivated to persuade me in any way.

Rationally, I know that that's impossible, yet... I can't shake the feeling that maybe it is possible?

"You're not the center of the universe."

My stepmom would constantly tell me this when I was a child, and although it has severely cut my self-esteem (even as an adult), I have to wonder how true it is.

I don't want to be the center.

I don't even want to be a side character, get me off this stage!

But maybe she always told me to throw me off their trail, so that way they can continue watching this sick form of entertainment.

No, no. That's crazy. Of course that's not real life.

And when I'm not following their script, and when I stray or do the opposite, they gaslight me. How many times has my stepmom told me that I was lying? How many times did he accuse me of things that hadn't even crossed my mind? Or when I admit to lying about one thing, suddenly, I'm lying about everything else?

Even today, I am told that I'm exaggerating previous abuse or that none of that happened. How are you going to tell me that didn't happen? Why? Because she's nice to *you? You* couldn't imagine her doing that?

It's a lonely feeling, not being heard by family. They can't accept the bad, or that mental illness is a real thing. Yet it's surrounded my whole family for generations, perhaps some of my sisters and I are the first ones to acknowledge it. Or maybe I really am the first one to genuinely not be able to 'suck it up' and live a normal life. And I fear that I will never have a normal life. Similar to Alice in Wonderland, I have lost my muchness. How do I get it back? Have I ever had it?

Mental illness isn't always disappeared by medication and exercise. It's easier to hear gossip and believe the rumors rather than just listening to the person who is drowning! How many times have I heard that my own family thinks that I'm doing hard drugs? How many times have I heard that I'm a porn star? A sugar baby? Freeloader?

Instead of just coming and asking me, they all choose to believe it and I am left...sinking in this crushing abyss, weighted down by their rumors and lies, unable to save myself. Alone, alone, alone. But isn't it better to sink alone than drag someone below the surface with you?

My heart is the only thing grounding me to this planet, lest my body float up and touch the clouds as I so desire. I want to let go, I want to leave, I want to go. The internal struggle is so loud that it thunders throughout the mountains and deafens all who are alive, truly alive, not just surviving.

Every mentally ill person has heard to just suck it up, go outside, get therapy, get sun. You are blinding yourself, giving yourself the illusion of control.

If one does all that, you won't have to suffer like me, is what you're saying.

I'm only sick right now because I'm not doing everything right.

I must not be.

Because you are, and you're not sick. Right?

But you have no control over anything. You can exercise and eat right yet still die from a tumor on your spine tomorrow. You can have a healthy social life, take the right vitamins, yet still suffer from depression. You are not in control over anything. You are truly at the mercy of the universe, and it scares people. You're not even in full control of your own body.

People are scared of roller coasters and airplanes because they're relinquishing all control, they're at the visible mercy of science and mechanics. But the thing is: it's like that all the time with everything, yet people pretend that that's not happening.

People give themselves this false sense of power and they let it cloud their vision. What exactly are you controlling? Humans have invented religion and taxes to keep up this charade that we control our own destinies.

Do you really think that the universe cares about it being 1:00am?

That there's a man in the clouds overwatching you and he cares more about you being gay rather than focusing on the millions dying of starvation or victims of human trafficking?

You have to pray all the time to him otherwise you'll get cancer like the bitch down the street that has never been to church.

Isn't that how it works?

You pray all the time, and you don't have HIV.

It's easier to blame the victim rather than truly come face to face with our vulnerability. Things happen, and it's more dupable to blame the victim than allowing the anxiety to overwhelm us. Because if one actually thinks about it long enough, how vast and chaotic this fucking universe is, madness will ensue, and consciousness will ebb from existence.

I would hope that anybody that truly believes in religion begs for forgiveness because if it is real, we are all going to hell. There won't be a single soul that escapes. We have all stolen, lied, committed sins that by an outside audience would deem too unforgivable. We only justify it because we know our true intentions, our authentic reasonings. and give ourselves the benefit of the doubt. This life that we all live is the only thing we are able to control, yet we still have no power over it and over ourselves.

Doesn't it scare you how easily your mind can snap? That small issue that is nagging you in the back of your brain...it starts to grow bigger and bigger until one day it's all you can see. It consumes you, it's all you can think about. It's overwhelming and powerful and nothing anybody says can deter you because you've seen it.

You know.

But it's in your head.

It's only real to you, but it's not real.

Nobody is safe from this. Not your friend, or child, or spouse...not even you. You are not safe from your own mind. It can turn against you. Maybe it's punishment or reparation. You must repent for your sins: every dirty thought, every idea of revenge or evil. God is not real, and maybe not even the devil...but I know that you wish they were. It would be easier to blame a single entity for your problems. To say that they are the ones that caused it...even though you know, deep down... that you are the transgressor, and you must be punished.

This retribution...your idea of hell that you imagine every time you see the word... you never think of it being your destination. And why would you? You're a good person: you do your taxes, you pick up after your dog, you take care of your family...

You're a good person...aren't you?

You think that your actions in the daytime are enough to outshine what you do at night. But I fucking see you. You are not concealed;

everyone can fucking see you. Just because you can't see me or the bigger picture or the signs doesn't mean that you are undetectable. And just because you're a fucking pebble in this pond doesn't mean that you're not polluting it with your poison.

But you brush it off today, you don't care. Why would you? You're at the peak of your lifetime, nothing can touch you. You can move your hand at will, you can change the appearance of your body, you can drive into oncoming traffic, you can do whatever you want. But really... this life is not your own. You are simply borrowing it, a rental vehicle meant to transport you to the next life... which will arrive sooner than you realize. You're only made of carbon, stardust, and ignorance.

To let them escape this wretched and sick world and send them to a peaceful afterlife is the ultimate gift. To hold the essence in my hand and catch it in my closed fist, lit up like a firefly, eager to fly away yet struggling against my fingers. Only to fly away at my whim, whenever that may be. Hours, days, centuries.

And once I bleed the life out of your so-called body, every mortal drop, every sin and thought and dream you ever had: past, present, future... when your body was clean, and your soul was empty... I wouldn't even close the eyes that you once had. Because eyes are stitched close when they're preparing the bodies so that they're not forced to witness their sins and offenses in the afterlife. But I wouldn't do that to you, to your victims, to the world. Your body forced to repent for the sins that you committed or ever thought of committing...

And really, when you think about it, this wouldn't be a crime. It's only a crime because the wretched cannot discern when it's a murder or a release. You think too small, too meager, and too petty.

I could tell, and I could do it. I would release you. A release from this cage that you are putting yourself in to appease everyone else. And maybe it's a good thing that you're in a cage because, honestly, you need it. Without it, you would lash out and rip anyone's throat you see with your teeth. You would destroy anything for the sake of extermination.

You don't truly see the value of a life.

But I do, and I can see how beautiful it is. How small and insignificant every person is. You don't matter. And that's beautiful. You are smaller than the grain of sand that is stuck to the bottom of my shoe.

You can be squashed out of existence, and it would be a blessing. No longer would you have to feel pain or cold or jealousy. Envy, rage, sickness... all gone in your eyes. You could live again, renew and start over, because surely you have too many sins to stack up against. You are disgusting and it's not your fault. It's not your fault. You don't know any better.

But I would be here to help you, to bleed the sin from your damned body, to catch your goodness that is ever shrinking in the meat suit you call home. You are immoral and guilty, but I could deplete your wrongdoings, swallowing your agony as my own and never once a complaint leaving my lips. I would do that, because it is my obligation. As a being that is more knowing than you will ever be in any of your potentially infinite reincarnations, it is a burden that I have no objections to hold against the universe, and certainly not against you.

To be angry at you would be as pointless as indignation towards a carnivore eating its prey. You're not resentful towards the lion that stalks a gazelle, nor the hawk that kills for its food. You're indifferent because you know that that's a fact of life, death is an inevitability that leaves you with no choice but to accept it. Why be angry at the inevitable?

# CHAPTER 6

The man is still, crouched, ready to leap at the first hint of danger. His eyes follow mine as I delicately make my way through the maze of rocks and treacherous footing. It's cloudy and the shadows of the clouds against the sky cast ominous doubts on both of us, surely. I saw him a mile away and as I started climbing towards him, he had not moved a single inch from his position. He's naked, so I feel less afraid somehow.

My feet are bleeding and leaving a trail of footprints, my humanity marking the rocks for...I wish: eternity, but in reality, only a few seconds until the waves lap them up. The only sound is the ocean, and while I know that I shouldn't touch the water, I feel a calling, a beckoning that is so sweet that it's hard to ignore and continue on.

A few times I slip but catch myself with my hands. I am raw and exhausted, yet he does not try to meet me halfway. Why won't he at least acknowledge me? Why am I still continuing this perilous journey with no idea how it will end?

Time is meaningless, but I fear that this jaunt has drained me my entire life, my essence of a human bleeding dry yet I still continue on. Hope is a forgiving sin that propels even the weakest of bodies forward through enmity, physically and emotionally.

I am feet away finally, separated by a single flat rock. I stop and stand there, facing him and not saying the first word. He stands up slowly, his body trembling—from fright? From weariness? From anticipation?

As we look at each other, his true semblance seems to come alive and materialize into existence. He's handsome, not a scar or blemish on his face nor body and stands tall. I start to feel an enigmatic suspicion that he is sizing me up; mistaking my spilt blood and abraded skin for weakness. He has the same expression of a cat about to pounce on its kill: a cocky hubris that hasn't failed him yet. I don't know how long he's been standing on this rock—it could have been his whole life—and as I look down briefly at my feet, I see the reminiscence of burnt ash that hadn't been wiped clean by the ocean yet.

I am not afraid yet. As I stand there, defenseless, his eyes start to light up, as if he were staring too closely at a fire and the whites of his eyes are reflecting the flames. In a flash, his eyes are consumed by two fireballs. I am too memorized to move, my body freezing on the spot at this sight. And just as fire does, it grows, consuming his face and traveling to his open mouth. Flames licking his face and swallowing all hints of his humanity, it grows bigger until it runs out of room on his face and starts blasting forward away from his body and towards...me.

Three horizontal columns of fire breathing to life and growing so large that it was inches away from my body. I am in awe, unable to move, unable to do anything but stare at this ... fire made of human mortality. I feel it start to cook me, running up and down the front of my body until it engulfs me, evaporating all the oxygen from my lungs and scorching every inch of me until I feel skin start to melt and drip down my bones. My eyes pop like grapes and run down my cheeks, liquid chunks fusing to my face and dissolving flesh until layers are gone and my skull is exposed to the furious inferno. My tendons are snapping like guitar strings and my organs are popping one at a time. My eardrums ruptured, blood dripping down on the inside of my ears to drown what was left of my cooked brain.

I could not see or hear in the traditional sense, but I could still observe my surroundings. I witnessed my body start to disintegrate back into ash, everything holding me together as a human being just...vanishing.

The pain was ever present, not a single moment forgotten nor forgiven. The only sliver of my brain left that was capable of thought prayed to anything that could help or end me—whichever came first.

I was being unraveled; every memory and thought fading, I was being expunged from my very existence. If I still had my esophagus (which had welded shut already), I would have cried out my last word. What it would have been is lost to the cosmos.

And suddenly, an ethereal force rammed into the incandescent man, forcing his body back and almost snapping his neck with incredible violence. The fire burned brighter and hotter as he cried out in pain, losing his balance on the ocean rock and falling backwards, his surge of hate no longer directed at me but aimed uselessly at the sky where his body lay flat. The flames slowly diminished, and his face became human again. He cowered like a child, arms raised above his head, tears and snot streaming down his face, sizzling when it came to contact with his once hot cheeks. He cried out apologies and excuses, anything he could think of to save himself. His body was shaking, fear choking his words until he was reduced to sobbing so loudly that the very sky shook and threatened to collapse.

I was curled up in a small ball, unable to move for my skin fell away with every movement. I was a charred skeleton, not even human anymore. I had no hair, no eyes, and slopping skin that barely covered what was left of muscle and bone. I was not alive. I never was alive, was I?

Tenacious—albeit gentle—hands touch my spine. Touching each vertebrae as if counting them, slowly caressing the back of my naked skull, trailing a finger along my vulnerable tendons and creating violin-like music by strumming them. The music swells louder, overpowering everything in existence and gifting memories back into my consciousness. With every note comes a new reminder of my existence here on earth, memories flooding in and emphasizing the good that had momentarily escaped my vitality. My body is a literal instrument, and it vibrates and hums out of my control, my seemingly last benevolence to the lovely cosmos.

I uncurl the husk of my body and face the sky. Before, it had been dark and overcast, but after the fire burned out, Heaven came alive once again. As if once the monster had been defeated, the sun wasn't afraid anymore and now it was free to bestow its own gift to humankind again. The clouds danced to the music of my body and the sunlight was truly hypnotizing; the world's heartbeat had begun to beat again, and it reunited with the beauty of the blue from the ocean once more.

I had spent all of my energy making my way to the fiend in good faith that it was my obligation, and now that I was frozen in eternity, my essence drained and vulnerability divulged to every being dead and alive, I had to wonder: was it worth it?

I couldn't see the entity—for she had no physical body—that had saved me, but I could feel her lying next to me, staring at the sky as if she were the one that had personally beckoned the sun. Maybe she had. I wasn't sure. And although my body was broken beyond repair, I felt...*human*. I wasn't the one that had felled the leviathan, but I had survived, unlike the victims before me whose only mark left in the world an ashed scar alone on some random rock in the ocean.

The agony was almost enough to kill me, but I turned my head to the once fire beast. He was still lying on his back quivering, the tantrum long gone and now could only be described as a petrified kid. He didn't have any physical wounds, yet he held himself as if in pain. He senses me looking at him and turns his head to meet eye contact. He's blubbering too much to speak, and instead holds out his hand to me, palm up.

My body mutilated and almost completely annihilated; I could not ignore his cry for help. I roll onto what was left of my belly and start to drag my mangled body, army crawling on my elbows. Tears were running down my face despite the fact that my eyes were still liquified. Blood is squirting out of the hole that used to be my lips, pus oozing out of every orifice, pieces of flesh dripping. What was left of me was falling apart, leaving a trail of what used to be my body, yet I couldn't keep my humanity if I refused this call for help.

After almost every inch of me had renounced its devoir as my human body and fell off my bones, I reached him. If I were to look back, I'd see a path of death and anguish and desolation. No strength left in my soul, yet I still find something in me to lift my arm up high enough to grasp that hand that had been held up my entire odyssey, waiting for me. Not an ounce of flesh left, blackened bone peeking through his unharmed hand when we intertwine our fingers.

We lay together, his body still in the same position he was felled in and my body perpendicular to his, unable to move any further even if I had wanted to. We are still until his tears finally subside and he is able to look up at the sky and truly appreciate its beauty, yet I have a feeling that he couldn't really see it.

When he speaks, his voice is small and childish, but the farthest from innocence the world has ever witnessed. I let him speak, unable—or maybe unwilling—to respond. Once he started talking, he didn't stop. And honestly, most of it was nonsense that was dense and short-sighted, but I was able to learn who he truly was from what he didn't put into words.

He tells me how sorry he is, how hurt he is, how many other people he's already killed with his tongue of flames. The anger building up inside of him is just too hot to keep in and he is simply not strong enough to keep it contained. I am not resentful of him; I just feel pity for him. And I realize that this is the first time that he has been touched by another person (although physically I no longer qualified as a person) for he incinerates all who are foolish enough to come close enough. He speaks of innocent blood being shed and how remorseful he is afterwards when he lays back down, yet the guilt doesn't stop him from exterminating the future victims that flock to him.

I could empathize with his loneliness, but his untapped anonymous fury was not understandable. What was the benefit of vaporizing people who could potentially help you? Because he was angry in that one second and acted villainously and now has to live with the combined guilt for the rest of his life? Was that worth it?

And I knew that although my body was failing me, I would never want to trade places with him. I crossed the threshold of life and death despite the inevitability that my body would face, yet he would not walk the easy path to help me. He held on to his physical beauty and safety but at the cost of benevolence. He believed that by destroying people first, he would stay safe. And to a certain point, he's right. He has stayed safe for millennia, older than the universe and the moon and the stars put together, yet he hadn't the chance to mature and truly live because of his fear. He was this... child in an old man's body and he looked human, but he was an unforgivable zealot too resentful and too foolish to listen to anything outside of his own head.

He talked for centuries without saying anything truly substantial. But I listened anyway and waited for my body to mend. In all those years, I never said a word to him because I knew he wouldn't listen.

The deity that had saved me came to visit occasionally. She'd lay next to me, and I'd feel the warmth radiate from her body, mending my bones and caressing my scarred skin. I'd feel all her goodness and we'd have conversations in my head, never speaking out loud because I knew that she could hear me regardless. But when she came, the fire ogre trembled with fear. He screamed and convulsed as if a demon were inside him begging to be let out. He'd plead and beg and cry, imploring her to let him be. We would both ignore him, his howling unheard as if he were an ant that just wouldn't understand that his voice was too small. He never dared to ignite his fire on either of us again, yet undoubtedly wanted to.

I wondered if she was transferring my pain to him when she was present, showing him the true hurt that he inflicted on my uncomplaining lips, but I never confirmed this. He never explained why he would cry when she was here, he would never talk about anything serious; just his frivolous affairs that weighed so heavily on his mind for some odd reason.

My body became stronger, my eyes were fixed, my organs functioned normally. Yet I still laid there with him, listening to nothingness in the form of words, unsure what would happen when I did get up. Seasons came and went, snow piling on my unmoving body, waves crashing over me and then icing, rays of unadulterated sunshine so hot that it sizzled my skin. The man would get up and pace often, leaving a trail of fire from the friction of his feet.

And came the day I felt ready to stand. I flexed my fingers for the first time in years, and then my arms. The spasms traveled my body and reignited the spark of life that lay dormant in all. Standing up, every joint popped and the pressure that was finally relieved rejoiced in song to the sky. The man watches, mouth agape and for once, not saying anything. I am many feet taller than him, and I have to look down to see him. How could I have been so wounded by a man that was inches tall? It's a wonderful feeling standing upright, and I stretch and silently praise the heavens. The once fire beast tries to speak, but I physically can't hear him, and I don't care enough to try to.

I stepped to the edge of the rock that had captivated me for so long I considered it home. I turn briefly to look back at the man that was destined to be forever alone, destined to never truly hear anybody besides himself speak, never had I uttered a single word to him. The water was unusually calm today and it silently invites me in. I raise my arms above my head and with little to no splash, I dive in and am free once again.

I gasp, eyes opening as wide as they go but I still can't see. I try to move my arms to the side, but they're stopped by... a wall of dirt. My legs do the same, and I am hit with overwhelming panic by this tight space. Showers of loose dirt coat my skin, stinging my eyes and choking my airway. I flail around, screaming at the top of my lungs until I am hoarse with rage and exhausted from the effort.

I lift my shirt enough to cover my face from the dirt and I start thrusting my hands and feet towards the sky, digging my fingers and kicking as hard as I can. The noise is incredible, and the earth shakes as if enraged that I dare try to save myself. The deep humming gets louder and louder the harder I kick dirt, and soon it's deafening. Roots, leaves, bugs, all are falling back onto me, threatening to suffocate and eat my body.

The sweat pouring off my skin mixes with the dirt and creates mud, swirling around my head and submerges up to my ears. I don't slow down for fear of truly drowning if I second guess myself. Seconds drone into minutes, minutes into hours. My shoulders are on fire and my body is weighed down from how heavy the loose dirt is. I'm digging and then pulling my body up, over and over and over again.

# CHAPTER 7

When I open my eyes to the real world—my second awakening to the real world—I am always genuinely surprised about how young I am. Spending centuries alone in your head and going through heaven and hell and everything in between seems like something that would take up all the time that existed in the universe, but I find out it only takes a few days or even hours in earth time. Are they dreams or dissociation episodes? Or a mix of both?

And I have had everybody tell me that my imagination is just too much, and I need to get a hold of myself. Don't you think I've tried? When I live through these scenes, I'm not just seeing it in a VR-type of setting. I am *living* and *experiencing* it as a whole.

Even small things (at the time) grow and build and soon it's the biggest thing you've ever seen and it's on public display so everyone can walk past and gawk at it. This...snowball of depression and insecurities, fear and paranoia, accumulating until it desecrates the unsuspecting town at the bottom of the hill. Emotions that just cannot be let go or ignored, despite the countless attempts of others telling me to just do it or how they got rid of theirs. If I could get rid of it, I would! I would! I would go out and buy a snow shovel right now! A flamethrower! Anything! Everything!

I am so tired of living everybody else's lives that I just want to sit under this oak tree and admire the sunset before the sun is extinguished forever and unable to rise again. I am tired of playing the part of everyone on this god-forsaken planet. I am tired of being good, evil, melancholy, childish, rude, forgiving, every single trait describing every single person. I am you, I am them, I am she.

I have lived the life of it already, reincarnating every time I die. I can see every single life of everybody in this universe, and maybe that is why my anger towards others is actually directed at myself, because I should know better.

When I die, the sun will collapse into itself, and the world ends as well. The universe has been birthed alongside me and will die alongside me. She cannot keep going on her own, and I do not blame her. I hold her hand and help steady her for we have a long walk ahead of us. That's the only seeming reason why I am saved every time I try to die. Because without me, everything ceases to exist. Saving me was out of self-interest.

I am forgetful (or purposefully ignorant) of the laws of mankind. I forget the rules that keep me out of prison, the ones that define who I am to society. How are we to know what keeps the policemen from banging on our door at 2 in the morning?

There are no consequences for my actions because I am not a part of your world. I am watching you through a television set. I am on stage, but I am not the one being watched this time; I am watching all of you right now. I am in a bubble that I do not want to pop, because when I do, my vulnerability and essence will bleed onto all of you, tarnishing it...marking it...shattering all illusions that you once thought were real. Why would I willingly annihilate your world? You are my children, and a mother does not readily kill her child. I protect innocence and pick you up when you scrape your knee. I don't want the world to jade you, but when it does, I am here to comfort.

I know that all my lives are connected because I am high enough in the sky to see it all play out. The signs that the universe shows me to tell me that I'm right, the divination that I have been gifted but unable to use for fear of devastating it.

I can feel every single emotion that you have felt, birth to death. Those memories that define who you are as a person are all mine, little trinkets of nothingness yet are the cache to me. Treasure? Burden? The actions that have unraveled your dreams and birthed a new beginning, all of it.

Every disgusting fantasy you have played in your head, your thoughts of vindication, hopes, dreams, nightmares, desires, I can feel every single one. I am feeling alongside with you; I am crying your tears, smiling your smiles, celebrating your victories, and grieving your losses. You can't or don't even know that I stand right next to you and hold up part of your burden, and you cry and maybe yell at me for not helping you, but I am! I am helping you! You aren't looking high enough; my arms are held up and shaking from your weight but you're too busy looking at my feet! Look at me! Look up!

But even the ferryman gets tired of going back and forth and seeing only the wholly good or complete evil in people and I don't want to know people anymore, I can't be around people anymore. They are always telling me how to live or do this or *this is how*, but I need to learn how to die and to stay dead. I don't want any more of this.

I am aware that this falls under the god-complex that some people exhibit. Isn't it? Aren't I? Am I?

And it's embarrassing, because I don't want to think like that. I love living in the shadows where nobody knows me, and I don't know them. I have moved so many times in my adult life and found new cities every year and I love it. Why would I be feeling this way?

And it's not as if I feel that I *am* God, I just start falling into the delusion that I am capable of this ...deity life that isn't human. I am everybody in this world, living not as if time were a linear line. As if this whole universe was created for me, by me, maintained by me.

Big-headed, isn't it? Once I am out of that episode, I can clearly see the world again.

I can hear my stepmom's voice echoing since childhood: "You are not the center of the universe."

I know that I am back in the real world, because those words are not a challenge brought on by the universe to trick me. In the real world, those are true words. And thank god for that, because even just being on stage is so frightening and intimidating. The dread of being in front of millions of people. The feeling of all these eyes on me, watching my every single move and judging...

How can I want to be in the limelight when I can't even look at myself in the mirror or the reflection of my body in store windows? I spend so much energy worrying about literally just being presentable. The minimum. How do I not look like a half-formed monster straight out of a horror movie!

I don't even look in the direction of a mirror for too long lest I call upon Bloody Mary and she rips my heart out and drains my memories and all the knowledge I have fought throughout many and many lifetimes to hold onto. I don't want to let go of anymore! I am losing everything that had once held great importance to me!

When I turn my back to the mirror in the bathroom, I can see out of the corner of my eye my reflection looking back at me. A few times, I have caught her out of mimic, body fully facing me as if studying me. Does it try to communicate with me? Should I listen to her? Will she take me with her?

Or if I accidentally catch my reflection in the mirror, sometimes I'll see myself as a skeleton. Literal bone without a single layer of skin or muscle or anything humane that would suggest that this reflection was once alive. There are no eyes, just two empty black cavities. There are no lips or tongue, no hair or even cartilage. How it was staying together and not falling apart, I'm always unsure.

I see the being with many faces. I am the being with many faces. I have...devil horns. To my right: a laughing face, evil and cruel, a chuckle that boils your blood. It flings itself at me through the mirror, but there is nowhere for me to jump back to, or escape, or even to cower in a corner and close my eyes.

Was this all I truly was? Or is this how others see me, and the veil has just been lifted from my eyes at last?

# CHAPTER 8

Emotions separate from my person. Not as if I were floating alongside, but in a way that if something happened to me, it wouldn't really happen to me. A lovely box that I can throw my *later*'s in, a junk drawer, a procrastination endeavor.

My cat. How many times have I cried over that creature? When she ran out of my apartment one night and was missing for a few hours, to say I was devastated would be an understatement. The times I was in a delusional state and thought I was going to prison and she straight to the pound, I cried so hard for her. How alone she would be, sitting in a cage not much bigger than she is.

But when I really think about it... when I self-analyze and I sit there and comb through the dark recesses of my brain that I never venture... I realize that I don't truly care. I should give her away so that I will never have to know of her death. No sickness, no injuries, all of it perfect memories that I can hold dear and swallow and keep safe from everything bad in the world that cares to defile it.

I know that I would never willingly leave her. The uncaring part of me that puts her in my box of *later*'s is lying to me and I would never discard her. She'd spend the rest of her life wondering why I abandoned her, and she'd always wonder why she wasn't good enough and I'll never be able to tell her that it wasn't her! It really was me! It was me!

There's a reason! Please let me explain! Please hear me!

It's the final snap of a photograph, pictured perfect to remember for the rest of time...and afterwards... ceases to exist. It dissolves, crumbles, powders, all of it in the blink of an eye...except me. I am left standing in a pool of black and nothing but the light of a star millions of hours away from me and the moon that only laughs...

What a sense of humor the universe has. What will be held against me and how much of a hypocrite I am will smother me alive, burying me in this Earth so that I may never reach the stars.

The image in my hand is the only thing keeping me grounded, the picture of what was, and the forever could've been. But it's only a picture, and I don't let it obscure my whole vision, I have things to see, places to be! I put it in my pocket and only bring it out when I'm sitting around a campfire with the shadows of flames drunkenly flickering, a hallucinogenic atmosphere so heavy that I forget how long I've lived and what my name is...

The voices and sounds that come into my brain...

Maybe I am just naive. But I guess we'll see. Aware of how wrong I am either way, if you are reading this: I am losing, if you are not: then I am losing. So why bother?

I notice the signs that are sent to me. They are a confirmation that is sent to only the ones that will actually listen. How many times has the universe tried to speak yet goes unheard? Does the resentment start to grow, bubbling below the surface and dormant until the right spark ignites a chain of reactions?

And so yes, I see the fucking sign, I see it. Why aren't I heeding it this time? It's literally written in my blood, a semi-permanent emblem that is constantly in my eyesight. When will it heal and disappear? I feel as if its's been on my hand forever, my body refusing to heal it until I truly grasp the meaning, until I fucking see it.

Don't I get any reprieves? I have obeyed for so long, too long have I done what others have wanted for me. Making decisions for myself but then getting talked out of it or convinced to do something else. I want to go my own way, my own freedom...what...? I can't? I'm not allowed to? I shouldn't? I wouldn't?

Of course, I'd rebel eventually, and then start to love the taste of blood in my throat. Give me more, give me more, give me...

That will be the end of the world—when Mother Nature cannot hold herself back any longer and rids herself of the toxins that she's been forced to swallow, excrete, and swallow again. The fucking wrath that all will cower in front of, the repercussions and justice that has been long time overdue, coating us all in a layer of our own filth and sin, forever silencing the last words formed on our lips.

It is the unknown...becoming known. The secrets are strewn all over in front of you, naked in sin and reasoning, the very comprehension as white and black obliged. Why wouldn't you want to look? It's the most beautiful blood bathed firework finale that will ever become. Most people are ignorant, walking past as if they weren't aware there were fireworks to the left of them.

This is the future of dreams, the one imagined by a person a century ago. Traveling to different worlds is a miracle. Too often, I am zooming out of the real picture, unable to bother myself with small details that ultimately don't really matter.

I see it 1000 years in the future, a biographical documentary style. They study everything that I do: from the things I do online, even under the anonymity that is assumed, to the private things I do right down to brushing my teeth. I see it as an Imax screen. Just as the people before us that we do today, even to something as simple as opening a wiki page, they had no idea. They lived their lives as real and not just a screen in my mind or the pages of a book. People are real.

Living as if I can see it numbered and on a timeline is so stressful, and it makes me question everything I do; small or big. Time isn't linear and so is not meant to be lived in that way, yet here I am. Here we all are, pretending it's not happening, and I don't know how to pretend anymore!

I can't have everyone thinking that I smell bad, I better shower. I can't have them thinking that I don't ever go outside, better go out to the store. It's consuming my mind and swallowing every thought I have, it's a pounding background, a painful reminder, unsought.

It's a different audience than the ones before. It is the future, my generation dead for centuries, when it is their time to judge. A chain of respect, wanting to look up what their dead relative was up to similar to us wanting to see if we're related to Pocahontas. But when they get to me... E... They'll have some weird and crazy stories. And I cannot tell if this is the feeling of shame that is being brought forward or if it is just anxiety.

The emotions one would think you felt the moment you knew you were dying are creeping up and suffocating me.

That feeling.

Wow.

This is...the worst.

My heart is drooping, and my body is heavy. If I hear a knock on the door, that'll be the spell broken. Or maybe it'll be as soon as I get up or see a real person.

Sitting on the kitchen floor, across from the dishwasher and the table, listening to him spew his delusions into the chilly air, all over me. Angry one minute and remorseful the next, it's a never-ending cycle. It's not all spoken to me, although I am the only other physical person there. At this point, I don't even hear all the words. Out of indifference, genuine boredom, who knows at this point. Or cares.

Everything is gray and bleak: the still-bare walls, the counters, even the windows were listless without any sunshine streaming through. A harmonious hell that nobody could hear me scream from—if I chose to scream. An infernal cohabitant that demanded every second of my attention in an attempt to cleanse himself of the unholiness that lay ever present inside him.

He asked me once why I'm not afraid of being alone. To him, that was the scariest threat and the ultimate punishment, yet could not help pushing people away first so that they wouldn't hurt him first. Isn't it funny what the lengths people go to to avoid fear? Isn't that the underlying reason for almost all of our actions? We push people away first because we're afraid of losing them so instead of ceding vulnerability by placing unpredictable trust in someone other than ourselves, we willingly burn the bridge with our own matches.

He is spending his last minutes alive attempting to infect anybody and everybody around him. But he's the one brewing the poison, drinking it unprompted, and then attacking all in his vicinity. Bystanders, children, doctors! It matters not!

He is the man that forced all hell down my throat while crushing my skull and ripping my heart out! He is the man that tried to incinerate me alive, calling out my name and watching as I drag my degraded body across the border of life and death! He is the man on the boat pulling me away from air and into the sand banks miles and miles below!

This man has been with me all my life, hiding away until the right moment to terrify, kill, destroy... How do I tell this wretch that I am not afraid to be alone because I don't want to bear witness to the sins and atrocities and unholy acts of evil? How do I tell the man that has violently put his hands on me and has tried to drain the blood of all who are unfortunate enough to try to be *human* and help him? The only way for me to keep my virtue, my *morality*, is by solitude, and he asks: aren't I afraid of being alone?

The humanistic urge to purge the badness and guilt and shame from your decaying body so that you might close your eyes forever asleep is suffocating me. I just want to truly rest in peace! How do I do this!

All that childhood rage and secrets wanting to spill, spill, spill. I am coming to the truth that I don't really care for anyone. This is all my 'normal people' mask that I have to do in order to be allowed to walk the streets and not just locked up in a corner somewhere that has been forgotten by the world.

Don't you realize I fucking know how my real face looks?

And that desperation to just have as much control over your emotions and actions as others seem to have and not been curbed by a refrigerator stepmom. Or an abusive boyfriend. Or the second abusive boyfriend.

I would get them to shut up forever, their last words a string of insults that they had tried to hurt me with. I wouldn't even wait for them to be asleep; I would want them to know the full power I had wielded against them that they had never even bothered to see. How strong I was but never visible until that very last deadly moment. Because I chose to not show it out of... love? Humility? Pity?

Call me a whore? Threaten me? Punish me for your Othello delusions? I would make sure that that was the very last thing you ever said.

Touch me?

The blood spilt from your neck would coagulate and choke your very airway before the bruises on my skin would even color. All this rage would only show up at that very last minute, before your organs shut down forever and your brain stopped working. Maybe you'd pray to your god, maybe you'd beg for mercy. I hope you do it out loud so that I can hear. I want to hear the fear that permeates your entire being and trembles your voice instead of the awful fury that you try to give back to the world. I would be doing the world a fucking favor. Nobody would miss you. Nobody would grieve for you. Nobody would even come visit your grave.

If you had one.

But you won't, because nobody will truly care enough to choose a marker, let alone pay for it.

You think that once you're dead that everyone will come to the realization that they were wrong! They should have given you another chance! We love him!

They won't.

They'll hear the news... and they'll have to sit down for a minute. They sit in stunned silence. They ask to verify, to make sure it's true. It's true. But there won't be any tears. They'll feel... glad. And then guilt, for feeling glad. But now they won't ever have to deal with your bull-shit ever again. They won't ever have to dread answering their ringing phone, praying that you aren't on the other line. They won't have to deadbolt their doors at night and set up that security camera because they knew that you were in their city that week.

They won't even tell anybody else outside of the family. None of their friends or neighbors will ever know, and they won't suspect any-thing because their behavior isn't off. They're acting normal. Why would anything be wrong? Why would they express grief over some-thing that just simply isn't sad? Now they can answer truthfully when a stranger asks how many children they have.

And until you have dealt with such poison, you will never under-stand the true relief of washing your skin free of it. The years that were polluted due to the toxicity that others couldn't see or compre-hend. The never-ending questions or, god forbid, statements of: "well, *I* would have just left!" from people who don't really care about the true story. Until your body has been scorched, bleeding until the blood runs dry, you will never be able to fully empathize with the agony, not really.

People preach of unconditional love yet when it comes time to lis-ten to their own advice, they evade their own spoken words. This is hardly new behavior, and there are hypocrites everywhere you look. But I suppose you can chalk that up to human nature. (Hi, I, too, am human... right?)

I have been bottling up all my words: the ones that needed to be said, desired, wanted, or even to just fill the silence. All those words that I so desperately wanted to be out in the air like everyone else's...right here.

When I picked up the bottle, I thought that I would just hold onto my words until the bottle was full and I could go and empty it in the sea or wash something anew. I thought that it was going to be an easy task: tip and pour. Empty again so I could fill it back up and restart the process. I've always admired the bottle. It's beautiful, and every night I put it by my bed so that I won't be a second without it.

But slowly, I began to realize it was a curse. It became heavy and cumbersome. I hated seeing it. It was a reminder of my failures and my differences from regular people. I lugged it around because I had to. It was so heavy, and my entire body hurt every single day carrying it around. Here and there, I would pour a little off the top. Sometimes more than others, but it was always a relief to get the top off, to uncork it for even a second.

Until I became so infuriated with it. The fact that I needed it, that I thought I needed it, the words that wouldn't matter if I spoke now because they hold no value but the solemn heaviness they still cast onto me.

I'm fucking ready to throw the bottle against the wall. To spill it onto the ground so that it may water the grass and reach the heavens, because it certainly won't do good down here. I need to throw it all amongst the stars and create a new constellation—or better yet, cast down those old stars into the ocean and replace them with all the hurt and anger and words and loneliness and pain I have bottled up so that maybe, just *maybe,* someone will look up at the sky and look at those stars and marvel at how beautiful they are. So a small part of me can be heard and validated. Because we all know that stars are just big balls of gas, yet we make pictures and stories out of them, we use them as a universal metaphor for something beautiful, we name them, we guide ourselves with them, we specifically go *out of our way* to get a better view of them.

But when I tried to pour some out...it's not a drop. It's a tsunami of an ocean of polluted water, blood, and broken glass. This...once beautiful bottle, carrying around sick and shame masquerading as a gorgeous vessel designed to want me to keep it all inside. More words than the stars in the sky, more sand on the earth, an infinite supply that I had been holding in my chest and then this bottle and now...?

I didn't want it. It was no longer beautiful to me, the way the belie enraptured me, the galaxies swirling in the middle, dancing and taunting me. I wanted those red ballet slippers off; I don't want to dance anymore. I am tired and this fucking bottle is being shoved down my throat to choke me and why won't my arms listen to my brain and just take this stained glass muzzle out of my mouth?

I want to be heard. So, I poured some of it out, not caring that it was drowning the room, house, city. I poured and poured until I was left unable to touch the ground, unable to see anything. I was ready to fucking drown and anybody who was close to me was going to be taken down with me to a watery grave.

*Oh dear, I do wish I hadn't cried so much.*

*Dear, I do wish I hadn't cried.*

*Oh, I do, I do.*

I couldn't do anything. I couldn't do anything. I couldn't.

I needed to relieve some of that pressure in that bottle of words and emotions and I could not comprehend anything until I could because goddammit it's my turn, it's my turn, it's my turn. Let me speak, I need to be fucking heard by something or someone and I need to empty some of this bucket, monsoon, ocean of emotions or it's going to come back down my throat and choke me until I gargle with blood and glass for years and decades and tear through my esophagus and rip through my body.

# CHAPTER 9

I am stuck in Adam and Eve's fucking garden. I am surrounded by beauty and all the colors you can't even imagine. But I am alone, too poisonous to be among others, not really wanting to leave my little palace. Do I choose the people, or do I choose a home? Why would I/ why do I feel guilty for choosing a home?

From here, I can see the end of the finish line for everyone else, but they're all scrambling around, blind and equally frustrated. Refusing to listen because they think that they can see. No, you fucking can't. How the fuck are you going to tell me that you know where to go, preaching as loudly as your little voice will carry.

You don't even know about waiting. What the fuck do you know about waiting in your little 80, 100, 200 years of living on this planet? How long have I been on this fucking earth, all along knowing each milestone and what happens when I get there, always knowing what's next...always waiting...

And you say that you've been waiting for forever. That's fucking nothing. That's nothing, and on one hand, I can empathize with you, but when you start trying to climb this mountain without a pack and relying on others for their kindness and then trying to ridicule me for carrying the right supplies, you can go fuck yourself. I've been sitting at this top for centuries, waiting for *you.* So, when you come here, don't start complaining and coloring the air with anger and self-projection.

Because this mountain is fucking peaceful and perfect and when you start ripping trees from the ground and stripping the green from the plants, I have to kick you out of this garden that you have been journeying to for all these centuries, all these millennia for nothing because you couldn't control your anger. All the way to the beginning, time unraveling and atoms unbinding because you haven't opened your eyes yet. You think the destination is this garden? You think it's a real place with real trees and real grass and living animals? That all you need are the coordinates?

And that's why you're still stuck on the trail, destroying all in the path behind and in front of you.

From this elevation, I can see it all. I can see you step closer and closer to the pit that's leading right straight back to the beginning of time, a hellish slide that will only circle you back to the big bang, an eternity rock to push up that mountain alone. I can see what is enticing you, the reflection of the garden mirrored and catching you like a bug in a fly trap.

And how can I blame you for wanting to go forward? Despite my warnings and your sense of judgment, you carry on; closer and closer to this pit of death that will just be the end of this lifetime if you don't heed my cries. I will not scream at you or physically block you, so if you choose to go forward, I will not stop you. Just as the parent has that obligation to let go, it is not my place to intervene with your fate because then you will never get to the right destination.

Will resentment start to grow inside you because of the view that I have? I am almost positive. But I have brought myself back down to Earth for the sake of others, and it is something that I do not want to do again. So, I will embrace the hate and the festering hostility and use it to keep myself warm at night while you are wandering the cold desert: too stubborn, too angry, to listen to anybody but the ones in your head.

And I can always quit the game and put ice on my wounds and sit in the nice, cool, clean hospital, with snacks and decent tv shows. I could tap out and it would be such a joy to release me from the eternal struggle, but it also would be even more incredible to hear that end bell, the ref holding up our sweaty gloves in celebration and victory! The rush of the crowd as they all leap up from their seats—excitement and adrenaline bursting and choking us all, the natural inclination to high five everyone around you, even strangers that for a moment: morph into people we would die for. A bullet or car blocked, not just a moral obligation to say that we would because that's what you should say about family because family is all that matters. Family is all that matters. Family is all that matters.

That's all we hear but blood isn't all connection and there is blood that I would not sacrifice for but others I would in no hesitation—whether a physically related connection or not.

Playing uno with my whole family, sitting around a normally big table but almost too small for how many people are present now. All laughter and joking and poking fun at each other. Snacks that are normally never in the house are being passed around and my stepmom is actually being nice to me because everyone is here and it's so great to feel peace in the scarred up angry bond we typically have.

Grandma's perfume is lingering in the air, the dogs are having a great time with all the energy in the room. The tv is on mute, the soft lights are on, music is playing. There's a lot of physical human touch: hugs, kisses, lightly punching, grabbing or tapping arms. Those nights always had desserts and we never have desserts at home!

Grandma loves to pretend that her uno card is the right color, so she confidently throws it down and switches the colors illegally. And maybe we were watching too closely or too casually, depending on the mood of the room at the time. Sometimes, she gets caught and sometimes she doesn't. But anytime we noticed, we all leaped up and smiled and chastised and laughed.

She'd giggle her beautiful laugh and exclaim the same thing every time: "I didn't mean to! I can't see the colors! It's too dark in here!" And it was always so full of laughter, and she'd be so happy, like a small child every time.

We'd all laugh with her and groan and exclaim our kid-friendly, not-really-angry curses out loud and then carry on but keep her under closer supervision.

So of course, I cheat in games. Whether in uno, monopoly, cards. But in a goofy, carefree way. The exact same way as my grandma. We laugh and chastise and the game carries on but I'm under closer supervision.

Maybe closer supervision discourages me, makes me rethink and not act so impulsively.

Am I acting out from my past or is it present day me? Where am I?

Sometimes I still really struggle against my strict stepmom after all these years. The things that were not allowed in that house are hard for me to do here in my own apartment. Whether they're good or bad rules: the necessary strict ones that parents should implement out of safety or the ones that were only breathed into life out of ridiculousness or pettiness.

Some things I do without realizing to avoid the imaginary drama that plays in my head without my permission. Some are purposeful decisions that don't say out loud that they're a product of my stepmom's teaching. No sweets for breakfast, which includes sugary cereal. Reasonable, right? Cavities, sugar crashes, etc.

All those months that I was floating in the water but letting only the rope hold me back, I tried to listen to her. I haven't had any of that for breakfast which is silly because I am an adult, and I should be able to have whatever food I want as long as I can afford it.

But also...health problems. You don't want diabetes or a heart attack too young.

Maybe I'll be a rare case of a young person to have a heart attack and logically I know that anyone can have a heart attack so that includes me— despite no family history, mostly clean living, and no major health issues.

*No movies that will rot your brain.*

Makes sense. Logical, right?

*Don't paint your nails red. You look like a whore.*

Ok.

*Don't take too long in the bathroom. I know what you're doing in there.*

I am too afraid. I know that you are always watching. I mean, He is always watching. Jesus? ...Right?

*There is nothing wrong with you. You're just lazy. You need to socialize more. Therapy is only for people who are sad. You have nothing to be sad about.*

Oh... ok.

*Never close any doors. You lost your privilege of privacy.*

They portray that a lot in the kid movies we watch, so a lot of parents must do that.

*Music is the only thing I know you like, so when you do something wrong: no music. No music.*

But music makes things quiet for me and I can finally think.

*This is how you do this. You're doing it wrong. How long have you been doing it like that? That is so wrong. You are so wrong. Why would you do it this way, what are you: stupid?*

I must be. I don't know.

*You are so lucky to grow up in my house. Any other stepmom would have kicked you out by now. You can't even brush your teeth right. Let me watch and tell you what you're doing wrong, step by step. You can't even wash your hair right at 13 years old. Let me stand over you and see how you're doing it wrong. Get in the shower.*

I'm embarrassed.

*You can't even speak right. I'll put your dinner in the middle of the table and when you say it right, you can eat.*

But I'm crying too much now, I can't say it. I can't say it. I am so hungry.

*You're talking back?*

You asked me a question. Ok...maybe there was a little teenage sass in there. Maybe I deserve this.

*Go to the backyard and pick out a stick and pull down your pants.*

We're outside, though. We have neighbors. They'll see us. Me.

*This stick broke on your bare skin. Get another one. If it breaks again, you'll keep going back and forth.*

The neighbors...

*You're chewing gum with your mouth open? Let me grab the wooden kitchen spoon. Pull down your pants.*

Ok. It's a gross habit. I deserve this.

*I've told you to stop running in the house or I'll lock you outside. Come on.*

But it's nighttime. It's snowing.

*You're talking about running away? I'll call the police on you and get you locked up for being crazy. I can do it. They'll never believe you.*

I do lie, whether because it is in my teenage rebellious blood or to childishly protect myself, so that must be right. Nobody believes me. I wouldn't believe me. Nobody believes me.

*I don't care that you don't want to do this. Do it because I am telling you to. You never want to do anything.*

But I'm getting dizzy and it's hard to breathe.

*Hurry up, people are looking. You're in the way.*

I just need a second, please, I can't breathe.

*If you kill yourself, you'll never get into Heaven. You'll go straight to Hell.*

I'm too young to know that. Why would I want to kill myself?

*I hate clothes shopping with you. You're so hard to get along with and you never know what you want.*

I'm embarrassed about my body.

*You're so good at swallowing pills.*

Thanks.

*The world doesn't revolve around you.*

*You're not the center of the universe.*

*Get over yourself.*

The internal rebelling that I must admit did a little bit ago and consequently seeing myself spiral and knowing that all I have to do is raise my head above the water but I can't do it but I can't but I should be able to but I can't...it's not that hard, everyone else can do it... so why can't I?

And then I do lift my head! And take a gulp of air! I can remind myself it's just cookies! I sound like a dramatic idiot who's losing it! I can hear myself!

There is always a lot of reflecting and cringing (just as almost every other person does), and I just want to go back and explain all my weird behavior to everyone I have ever come in contact with.

I was weird because this was happening in my life! Or I chose to act like this because I thought *blank*, ya know? I was a weird, fucking kid, but especially in middle and high school. I was being drained at home—bled almost every morning, afternoon, and night that I was there—and it made my whole school years gray and lifeless and I just couldn't do it and even when I was openly happy about something, I was very aware of the heaviness of the mask and my body always being tired.

The brief sudden memory flashes that happen every once in a while without my permission that leaves me shaky, and I just want to erase all trace of me from everybody and everything; scrub it all clean and disappear without a single trace or emotion.

I don't even want people to know my name. I don't want people to remember my face.

All those book reports and analyzing everything in the story plays in my head every day. She stays up late because night is the only alone time in a house full of half a dozen people. She must always flush with the lid down because germs are bad and that's only logical, right?! She sleeps on her belly with arms underneath her body to stay warm because her comforter was taken away as punishment but it's so cold in the house and she's been so cold her entire life. She's always been so cold, I've always been cold, I'm so cold.

I could live in this little bubble of stability and tranquility...the same thing every day. Waking up and knowing, basically how it's going to end. Laying my head down on the same pillow with the same thoughts and empty dreams.

That's what's expected. That's what my grandparents and aunt want for me. That's what's expected of me. I should have a good job and a husband and a modest place to live with a pet and take occasional vacations, get into politics and know senators and whatever depressing event is happening on the news this week. I should be visiting my family every holiday, always in a great mood and keep conversations going and end everything happily and fly back.

I know all the shoulds and the expectations that weigh me down so much.

All I have to do is raise my head above water.

I had the same upbringing as everyone else, right? Everyone else can do this and not freak out: years of the same type of job, always waiting for those few vacation days they allow themselves each year after they've saved enough. Food and normal dinners every night, normal friends and normal relationships. Do your taxes, get a good car, understand enough to carry on any type of conversation, don't freak out like a crazy person, because everyone is expecting you to be normal. Normal, normal, normal. The family isn't expecting a millionaire by Christmas, but normal is the bare minimum. You've got to be normal, everyone else can be normal. Everyone else can handle their emotions and not feel sick or anxious all the time. Nobody can see the things that you're seeing because they're normal and maybe if you tried a little bit harder, you too, can be normal. You must not be trying hard enough. It's easy...everyone else can do it.

My aunt tells me that I'm too hard on myself, that she's proud of me no matter what I do. She says that, but...I know that deep down: she's disappointed. They're all disappointed.

This is the little girl they raised. They poured their sweat, blood, and tears into her. Into me. At 2 years old, I almost got grandma arrested, my dad drove me across the country straight through. They spend lots of money on toys and gas and food and they're so full of memories of me and some of them are good and some are bad but they're all looked back on so fondly and equally as cherished.

And I can't remember any of the memories. They tell me all these childhood and teenage stories and I can't remember and it's like they're remembering another version of me because it's not in this version of me but I want it to be! I so desperately want it to be! Because I love my grandparents and aunt and dad so much and I want to be that version that they think I can achieve.

And when my aunt tells me that she loves me every few days on a text message, they are my lifeline. But it fucking hurts to hold onto and it's hard to respond sometimes because it means so much to me and I want her to never stop but also don't want her to feel obligated to do it and be annoyed that she feels she has to do it or I'll kill myself (again).

It's like all those things that should be helping me to the top are actually weighing me down, but if I say this out loud, it just sounds like I'm a brat who isn't grateful and always being side eyed and hardly being believed starts to get to a person. To me.

I didn't remember writing on the mirror, but I must have because my stepmom is yelling at me about it now. I do remember her calling me ignorant and I asked my dad the next day what that word meant and him (bless his heart) telling me it meant something great.

I took off the flip flips literally minutes before she arrived, and she was so angry because they weren't supposed to be off. She thought I was walking around barefoot, gardening, but no, I wore them and just took them off as I kneeled down because I didn't want to break or bend them. Spoonfuls of hot sauce poured down my throat until the bottle was empty isn't deserved. I don't deserve this. I don't deserve this? Maybe I do deserve this? I do deserve this. I deserve this.

The curse of the Virgin Mary. No, I didn't have sex, but I am with child! The false guilt applicable makes me feel extra crazy. I second guess everything I do and say. If I don't do ~~something~~ everything right, I get...in trouble. With people in real life or the ones in my head, I cannot even bring forth a memory of silence. What does it sound like? Is it freeing?

Maybe I'm always wrong, adopting my memories and twisting them in the Pensieve until they're spotty and almost unrecognizable out of guilt and shame.

Who am I? What if everything that I am is wrong?

Maybe this isn't even reality and my brain is out in the middle of the ocean, yet my body is here on Earth, creating havoc and acting crazy. What if none of this is happening?

This could be my limbo.

Dishes are done, laundry is drying, floor is vacuumed ...but what if that's because everything is put back to normal and I am just seeing ghosts from and in my memory: a past and future creator.

Limbo...Nobody and nothing holding me back. Everyday has the potential of being the same. The spell is broken when I do something different: leave the house, library, store, walk, drive, uber, bus. The sun doesn't seem to shine on days I don't go outside, and that's crazy because it's Florida and every day is sunshine! The sun isn't keeping her rays to herself until I go out to bathe in her beauty, is she? Maybe...she is...?

It was tugging me in the opposite directions so strongly and only serves to have my arms pulled out of their sockets and ripped from my body. Stuck in the same position I was from the beginning but with less pieces of me. But I don't have much to begin with, so please, I—

It's getting a little harder to breathe, each breath tightening, tighter than the last. I'm a little lightheaded, weak, tired, but if I lay down, something bad will happen. (Textbook answer to a crazy person but really, it will happen this time and it's not all in my head. Right?)

I don't want to be here. I don't want a body. I don't want to be here. I don't want to be alive. I don't want to be here, I don't want to be here I don't want to be here I don't want to be here. I don't want to be here. I don't want to be here. I don't. I don't want to be here. I don't want to. I don't want to be here. I don't want to be. I don't want to be. I don't want to be. I don't want to be. I don't want to be.

I'm fucking drowning and my head is being held down and I can't breathe and I don't know what to do. I've been staring at this half flower for hours now. I'm so tired, but every time I close my eyes, I panic because I can't see, so they open anyway.

I am so tired. I stare and stare until every single detail is etched in my memory and every petal and stroke and color means something important and I understand what it means but I don't understand why yet so I must continue my forever-forced dance in my red slippers. I am so tired but I am so afraid to close my eyes. I am afraid that this is not real. What makes it real? Why do I keep hearing the words: *it's all in your head*. Is it true?

All the cliche things that people...victims, crazies...say just fall out of my mouth, dripping like honey, attempting to cover my wolf legs with the fleece of a dead sheep at my feet. I don't know how this blood stained my teeth! I don't remember killing the king but I must have because my hands are red and the crown is on my head but I don't remember! I look down and see nothing amiss but when I look in the mirror, it's only a skeleton looking back. Everything is stripped and my thoughts and vulnerabilities and memories tumble out and everyone can see them and pick through them like a sad garage sale on a lazy Sunday morning. I want to keep them safe, I want them back to me, I don't want them left to the wind. I don't want to lose any more, please, please, please, help me pick them up, please...

I am going down the road. After staring at my own knee for over an hour and then seeing everything as it truly is again (?), it's clever to use white and beige to signal to the audience of stability and boredom, a calm horizon of purity and elysian. And of course, the most important color you can use to pop is red and I cannot continue because I am just too tired...

To taste the colors in the paint and feel and know every detail and its backstory and reasoning is intoxicating and I imagine it as a dance between the two of us, a ballroom waltz around the stars and through the galaxies. Different, but not so much that love pours out of their shoes and leaves behind a milky way galaxy. Their dance immortalized and prophesied in the stars, a story that seems so far away but really, when you think about it: the sun just rose, God just created the Garden, and the Big Bang just spilled over and flowered into a colorful existence.

I am swimming again. Good and bad.

# CHAPTER 10

Sleeping is hard. I keep seeing/sensing someone over me. I get all tangled up in my blankets from the constant urge to move and I can't tell what is real or not.

I see bugs. Someone is in my doorway. I see a face. I see someone on the ceiling, laying down as if opposite to laying in a bed. My reflection? Someone else's reflection? I see a hand under my covers, moving the blankets. Cockroaches run all over my body, darting out of the way when I slap them, but I'm never fast enough. Shadows move in and out of my peripheral vision.

The more stressed I am, the more I see. I see spiders, a little kid, a cat, a person. I am unable to tell if I am sleeping or if I am awake, and I do not know why dreams are so vivid. Sometimes I can tell when I am sleeping. But during the day, I cannot tell if I am awake. Am I really here? Is it in my head? Which is worse?

I am starting to choke, each breath reluctant to fill my lungs.

This is...the worst.

My body is not mine for much longer and almost too heavy for me to control.

My chest hurts as if I've been running for decades. My lungs are heavy and full of non-existent smoke, each breath painful and reminding me that I only have one airway and that I must make a stoma at the base of my throat, a hole to breathe out of because my current airway is about to fail. I've seen a couple YouTube videos of it being done...maybe I can do it. I think I can, it'll help me breathe.

The rational part of me knows that I shouldn't, but it's such a tiny whisper and the rest of me is screaming that there's no oxygen getting to my brain and I can't breathe if my throat has collapsed in on itself, can it, now?

My heart hurts, a sadness that is so deep within me that I can't even remember the original reason any longer.

All of my actions leading up to this moment don't feel like mine. That was another person. It must have been, because I don't just 'feel' emotion. I get swallowed by them, engulfed in the strongest wave and so I cannot just 'get over it' even though I try because that's how it should be. That's how I should be, that's how it should be. Where are my memories? They are being lost and forgotten, blown away by the wind.

I have to guess that my need to over explain and backtrack my thought process is to see if I am going crazy again. Because I can't fully remember the complete emotions when I am the other. When I am normal and touching grass, I don't (or can't) remember the complete emotions I felt during my prescription medication overdoses. The psychosis that followed it, the dreamlike resurfacing, seeing things that weren't there. I felt the full range, one by one, dowsing me in each flavor of the rainbow.

But what does water feel like on my skin? When I am dehydrated and shriveled from the sun, why can't I remember how water feels? I know that I am starting to touch the surface of crazy. I feel the water on my hands. I need to pull back.

But why? Because my family doesn't want me there? My friends are worried? But it's my life. If I want to swim, I should be able to. I'm responsible about it. I set up auto-pay on everything and direct deposit and feed the cat and I have enough savings and—

Maybe that's the best metaphor to describe all this: an ocean of crazy. You've got the dry people on the beach: comfortable, able to see the sky. The water is nice too, though, you can sit on the shore. The farther you go out, the lonelier you become. You're more vulnerable, slower rescue time if you start drowning, currents, sharks, if anybody even notices. But you could be a great swimmer, so you're confident and can swim out to the buoy and put on some goggles and snorkel and look down into the ocean floor.

It's beautiful, isn't it?

Nothing you've ever seen before! A window glance into a slice of heaven, you think. What would make the experience even better though? Maybe if you get a closer look at things. Hold your breath and dive to touch the natural treasure.

*But it's dangerous.*

It'd be a great experience,

*You could die.*

But I shouldn't be afraid to live.

*You need caution in your life.*

Over and over again, the whole court of arguing and justifying plays in my head when I need to make a decision. Sometimes it's too strong and loud that I have to walk away and skip whatever it was. I am both sides and neither. One at a time. Simultaneously.

I have a foot in the deep sand miles below but one of my hands is touching the air, grasping at nothing but refusing to be stilled and leave the sun shined air.

What is the line between delusion and justified fear? Why can everyone else see it but I can't? I feel a thousand miles away, as distant as a star, which one could envy from afar for its beauty and shine but not be able to see how lonely it is and how the star had a favorite person but sizzled and faded out—years, decades, centuries too soon. Now I am alone in the sky. Part of the landscape and not necessary alone, but...being on a boat in the middle of a hurricane.

Other times, I'm not a single drop of water. Occasional blissful moments, I am in the desert! Not really here, so not really caring or needing to pay attention to the actions that this body is choosing to do on its own. I am not a single drop of water. I am not a single drop of water.

I am not.

That's when I can poke the bear back again, when I have the courage to dart my fingers around its swiping paws that will slice me into ribbons should I be too slow and pluck one of its hairs.

Sometimes it's too enraged to feel pain, so it's for nothing. Most of the time, it makes him even more mad. But I have the satisfaction of knowing that I got a hair! I got a hair! I've got it! And now I can hold it up and relive this small victory, a small tether to the real world. Or maybe it's a gateway to hell.

I do try to remind myself that it's a material I don't need and I'm being silly and ridiculous. But I love the memories and the instant flashbacks to that moment's emotions and adrenaline. My desire for selective control? A consequence of something that shouldn't even bother me because I'll never use this hair as a weapon, turning it onto others as it has unto me just a mere second ago. It came to me as a sword—for defense or offense, I am sure I wield the choice—but I shall only use it as a pen so I may be the only one to bleed from it.

I can't move my body, but I am tiny and everything around me is monstrous and huge. Then it alternates, and I am the monster too large for this tiny world around me. Anything I grab slips out of my fingers like slime, and then suddenly hardens itself and forces its way out of my grasp. I'm on a roller coaster in my head and it's hard for me to get off when I'm strapped in and screaming, yet the ride starts anyway. I can't control my body but I hear people talking to me and I have to keep pretending to be ok.

They don't understand why I snap and get angry or upset at the smallest thing. I am so wound up and tight inside my own body; trapped in a sarcophagus hundreds of feet below and my rescuer wants to push my release a few extra years because they want to talk about the weather.

*I can't breathe!*

I want to scream, but they keep scolding me every time I interrupt them.

So, I lay, arms crossed over my chest, in a cavity too small for me, bugs crawling on my skin and feasting on the spilt, stolen blood, silently waiting for the lid to open so I can take my first full breath. Doomed...or lucky...?

It's a ... different type of feeling to be put into the game, a humanistic emotion that connects me to the world and to every single person again. I am real again.

I have been so much larger and looking down at the board and playing without much interest...but now... I've been shrunken down. I'm in the game. It's incredible. Suddenly, I'm overwhelmed with anxiety about ruining my life, grief if I lose my cat...it's all becoming real to me again. The cloud of smoke that follows him has left a strong, dream-like hazy filter on everything. A magical spell that blankets the world but for some reason, only I am put under.

It's an alluring hypnosis, and he just went a bit too long staring at the sun, getting too close to the sun. Complete blindness, looking at that star every day for years because he thought he was more angry and bigger than the sun, mistaking her shyness and silence as weakness for the inability to fight back.

So she bit him. Attacked him. Clawed at his eyes, vaporized any trace of what was left of his face. If he was going to use those eyes to try to dominate and conquer the whole world as Alexander the Great had attempted to do, then so shall his downfall be just as great.

And now I will have to wander the crowds again. All black and white and gray, my first bright color I've seen has danced right out of my reach. Brushing my fingers and leaving a warm tingly feeling that's blooming and spreading to the rest of me but just as quickly faded away. No color in my vision again.

My arms fall back to my sides, frozen in pain and shock at the sudden aurora that had sparked everything to life, animating as beautifully as in Sleeping Beauty when the fairies wake everyone up. The once stilled crowd moves again, walking pointlessly but not necessarily care-lessly.

His essence, his being, his soul, his very person was brushed sap-phire. Everything he touched turned, similar to King Midas, just as beautiful. When you're a single color, you start to diminish and fade...taking all the hues with you and disappearing them from the world. Truly a selfish act: kidnapping it for yourself and never giving it back. It turns melancholy and dismal everywhere you go, and what probably may have started as a gift, only turns into a life sentence of never seeing a true color again, only blue. Only blue. Only blue.

It was the color of the sky, the ice under your feet, the birds you pass by every day without a second glance. It was the ignored beauty that people don't look at because it's always been there. Of course, it's dis-regarded. But even the original beauty starts to fade away, and it starts to turn into an ugly color; the color of the isolated snow piles in the corners of parking lots, the color of the spilled coffee on the sidewalk that everyone takes care to step over, the color of the cut flower dying in someone's living room, forgotten and its worth no longer valued, each petal dying and browning as the hours pass. Dropping one at a time, a collected pile of time and death surrounding its base, intending to stay put for all eternity until some soul takes pity and trashes it so passing eyes no longer have to look upon it.

How long does a color stay beautiful? How long until it's faded and gone?

Why do I keep looking for blue? Why am I going out of my way to search for this color? I don't want to see it; I don't want anything to do with it. Fuck blue. I'm tired of it taking up all my vision, blinding me to the others. It used to be just a color to me. It's no longer just a color, and I am unable to even look up at the sky for fear of it swallowing me whole and retrenching my entire world...blue being the last color, the last thing I see. Truly, a horror ending that would deem me passage to the pits of hell where I am trapped for infinitude.

I don't have any energy to hide the real me, so here I am. 30 feet taller than everyone else, all colors on me, standing still because much like Steven's t-rex, their vision relies on movement and my facade is just so heavy to carry right now and so here I am... living amongst the empty husks on autopilot.

So here I am.

With the cocoon feeling of being swallowed whole in the belly of the beast, knowing I'm fine but can't immediately escape is sedating, yet fills me with anxiety and dread that sinks my stomach and pulls my legs with a heaviness that sucks me dry of all nutrients that are in my body and brain, both past and present.

The ever stretching to reach something but never reaching it. The people you see and the emotion that follows it is surely real. Of course, it's real. How could it be? How could it not be?

Like a hazy dream or looking through the wrong end of the telescope, destined to look at the stars but getting all turned around and somehow, I'm looking at the ground that's right in front of me but I can't focus the lens.

*But you're using an expensive piece of equipment meant to look at the galaxies and planets and stars! How could you not see anything, dummy!*

I don't know what I'm doing wrong! My feet are stuck in the ground below me, I cannot move. I want to see what everyone else is looking at, I just cannot move. I cannot fix this. I can only outwait this adhesive, because surely it must disintegrate eventually, right?

I AM ABOUT TO SLICE off the pad of my right thumb :) there is a ...layer that is not meant to be there and I can't get it off with soap or scissors, so a knife shall be next. I need it off of me, I want clean hands again. I'm about to cut it off. I don't want to feel it anymore, I can't keep feeling like this, why is it on my thumb!

I don't want to cry over blue spilt milk. I won't. I shouldn't. I can't.

Blood seems to be the only acceptable payment. Think of something bad? Slice something. Spiraling? Slice. Think of something I shouldn't be? Fucking. Slice. It. Off.

But I'm controlling myself. It's baby wounds, barely a scratch.

Calm down.

I haven't cut myself in years, nor had the desire to, but this time around is...different. I need blood.

Is this really happening? Or is this in my head? Is the universe truly mocking me or is the folie au deux bleeding into me? Is this real? If it were, I'd feel the blade. But I don't, and I watch in the reflection and it's like a movie and I am just watching a character slice her belly.

Why do I avoid reflections all the time but today I can look? Is it the red? It must be the red. And I fucking love it, I want to drown myself in it, swallow until I'm no longer thirsty and heal myself and submerged until the pain is gone and my flesh is new, a dip in the river Styx to cleanse and burn off all this dirt and sin I have touched upon.

How do I pretend to be ok? When do I get the chance to explain myself after everyone asks me questions and then immediately impales me, never bothering to hear the last words I gurgle through my blood, the words that would have cleared my name, if only they listened to me.

I created my own red, my own blood. I needed that red to be grounded again, because fuck you, so of course I needed to see red again.

To justify? To vindicate or punish or even just to acknowledge the feelings that have consumed me but are invisible to everyone else, apparently.

I looked into my reflection's eyes and saw a degrading leash. I wasn't going to be told what to do! All I have done in my life is respect the fence! I know where that line has been my entire existence, I know very well that I'm capable of crossing it. Ha! A 6-foot piece of wood that thinks it has the power over me to stop me? I could cross in a heartbeat if I truly wanted.

So of course, I needed blood. I didn't go deep, because the point wasn't pain or to hurt this body, I just needed to understand and respect red again. But I didn't feel it, and it was just my reflection! I haven't cut myself in years! I don't do that! I don't want to hurt myself! I just needed that red.

Or I'll slice off my pinky toe with a butcher knife and rubber mallet, I'll measure twice, cut once. If I go to the mental hospital empty-handed, that's not very polite. I need to gift them my blood—the purist payment and a sacrifice you cannot fake. If I don't, they'll take one look at me and not believe me. Nobody else has ever believed me, I need to show them that I really need help and everything has a price. Here is my payment! Here is my blood! Please help me!

It's the reaching for it, the ready set—all in good faith—or I'll be sinking right back to the seafloor. Everything is blurred and gray and the wind is pulling in every direction but if I let go, I lose everything. A tornado that lasts for all time, God's favorite cat and mouse game: tv static disfigures my vision, electricity arcing and dancing through the air. I can't breathe. The only thing reaching for me is him.

But once the winds die down so I can open my eyes again and look around oz...finally I'm understanding the true, unencumbered perfect being: a petal of the violet, a symphony of answers from puzzles I have left uncompleted for centuries.

It is that first breath of air as you toe the line between dream and reality, unsure of the tangibility but assured that the very ground below is real, it's real, it's real, it's real, it's not in my head, it's not in my head, it's not in my head.

The perfect and most beautiful flower on the tree that pauses time itself to ask if you're sure that you want to pluck or keep walking past so that everyone else following also has a piece of art to have the choice to look as they pass or not.

The first three notes of your favorite song, that first bite of food that we cooked and danced and created out of nothing. The momentary stability on this spinning rock in empty (?) space, the traveling through space or time or maybe it's just a forest but through this kaleidoscopic high, the song of the birds and trees and Gaia herself calling out, it's hard to separate reality... or maybe I just choose not to.

*Isn't it all in my head?*